Dor

MR. JAY JAY
BEST OF BOTH WORLDS

To have had the opportunity to observe such a wonderful
example of freedom in the true sense of the word was an
extraordinary experience: "the best of both worlds," as
viewed through the eyes of a totally free and
unequalled creature.

Note for Librarians: a cataloguing record for this
book that includes Dewey Decimal Classification and
US Library of Congress numbers is available from
the Library and Archives of Canada. The complete
cataloguing record can be obtained from their online
database at:
www.collectionscanada.ca/amicus/index-e.html
ISBN 1-4120-4161-9
Printed in Victoria, BC, Canada

TRAFFORD

Offices in Canada, USA, Ireland, UK and Spain
This book was published *on-demand* in cooperation
with Trafford Publishing. On-demand publishing
is a unique process and service of making a book
available for retail sale to the public taking advantage
of on-demand manufacturing and Internet marketing.
On-demand publishing includes promotions, retail
sales, manufacturing, order fulfilment, accounting and
collecting royalties on behalf of the author.
Book sales for North America and international:
Trafford Publishing, 6E–2333 Government St.,
Victoria, BC V8T 4P4 CANADA
phone 250 383 6864 (toll-free 1 888 232 4444)
fax 250 383 6804; email to orders@trafford.com
Book sales in Europe:
Trafford Publishing (UK) Ltd., Enterprise House,
Wistaston Road Business Centre, Wistaston Road,
Crewe, Cheshire CW2 7RP UNITED KINGDOM
phone 01270 251 396 (local rate 0845 230 9601)
facsimile 01270 254 983; orders.uk@trafford.com
Order online at:
www.trafford.com/robots/04-1968.html

10 9 8 7 6 5 4 3

To my Mother and Father,
who taught me to appreciate nature

Acknowledgements

Special thanks to my children and friends for their help
and support of this project.
To Henry Oden, an exceptionally knowledgeable editor, for
his expertise in the final preparation of the text.
To Richard Whitmore for his cover photograph of Mr. Jay
Jay perching on my shoulder.

CONTENTS

MR. JAY JAY
BEST OF BOTH WORLDS

By
DOROTHY HICKSON DUNN

Chapter One

The Rescue

It was the twenty-sixth of May, gloriously bright and warm, a day for renewal and a new beginning. The violent storm of the night before had ended and all was well with the world. I was a happy, contented person, not searching for nor anticipating that today would be a new beginning for me, the start of an odyssey that would bring me joy and tears, knowledge, compassion and understanding.

My yard is a place of special delight. It is landscaped with shrubs, flowers and fruit trees carefully selected to provide shade, nesting spots, food and shelter for birds. Three magnificent oak trees provide shade for the house and grounds. The kitchen window overlooking the side yard and rock garden is where I collect my dividends on the time and effort invested in placing bird feeders, and birdhouses about the area. The rewards from this effort are visible in an abundance of nature's glory, far exceeding the investment and repaying me many times over.

The previous evening, a fast-moving storm passed through our area. It started with thunder in the west, followed by lightning that brightened the overhead sky. The thunder rolled again and again, rain pelted the windowpanes and rooftop, beating like bird shot. The wind raced through the distant woods. Suddenly, the storm intensified and moved closer. Wind assaulted the trees, swaying them back and forth, whipping their branches toward the ground and again springing them upward. As the downpour continued through half the night, I worried about all the birds in their exposed nests.

It had been a rainy, cool spring. Conditions had been unfavorable for the many birds attempting to establish and nurture their families. I had been especially interested in a pair of bluebirds that were occupying one of the bird houses in the backyard. The morning brought blue skies and a sunlit yard, filled with cardinals, mockingbirds, chickadees and blue jays. My bluebirds were busily feeding their babies—a good sign.

Heidi, our German Shepherd, new to our family, was in the yard, trotting here and there, exploring the damp grass, when she suddenly stopped. She had detected an interesting scent. With her ears standing upright and tail wagging, she started licking something on the ground. As I looked through the window, I could see that whatever she was licking seemed to be moving on its own, and I ran outside to see what it was. There on the grass, nudged by Heidi's nose was a damp ball of down: a baby bird, tossed from the nest during the storm. The combination of wet grass and the dog's exploring tongue had frozen this fledgling into a sculpture of sodden misery!

Our gentle Shepherd had given the little bird a thorough face washing but didn't seem to have hurt it. What to do now was the question. My first response was that maybe I shouldn't interfere with nature. While I pondered this issue, the baby bird needed to be dried and nourished. I carried the helpless creature into the house and placed him on a warm bath towel. Before long he was fluffy dry and his bedraggled appearance turned into a plump body covered with gray down, adorned with a little stub of pinfeathers for a tail and a set of fragile, wobbly legs. He seemed to be healthy and I carried him back outdoors.

I thought the bird was about two weeks old. Because he was young and unable to fly, I looked for his nest. I first searched the pear tree in the side yard, a favorite nesting-place of our local birds. No nest. Then I listened for the sound of concerned parents. Still, no nest; I could not find it anywhere.

The only alternative, I thought, was to place him in the tree. That would give him some protection from predators and perhaps his parents could find him there. I located a branch in the pear tree that I believed his tiny feet could grasp. Very gently, I placed him on the limb, hoping his toenails could cling to the bark, and slowly withdrew my hand so he would not be startled by the movement.

I watched while he struggled to maintain his balance on tottering legs. He lost his steadiness and fluttered to the ground. I picked him up, repeating the process until he gained his balance and seemed comfortably ensconced on the limb. I left quietly, hoping the parents would soon find their offspring. I believed the mom and dad were in the vicinity of the yard or nearby woods and would hear his distressed calls.

I watched his progress during the day, making my final inspection just before dark. He was in the same tree but had moved to a higher branch. Birds prefer a night roosting spot that is sheltered and located a good distance from the ground. This gives them more protection from predators and may be instinctive.

At daybreak the next morning, I ventured outside to check on the little bird. He was not there. I searched carefully the entire area underneath the pear tree and shrubs but could not find a trace of the tiny fellow.

Had the baby been a meal for a stray animal? Or

had the parents not liked his scent? I have been told that birds do not take care of offspring who have an unfamiliar odor. If this bit of folklore is true, the outlook for the baby bird was not good. He not only smelled of human scent, but to make matters worse, he had been licked by the dog!

As I walked slowly to the house, I blamed myself more and more for not giving the orphan bird a home. Yet I was not certain that I was prepared to become the surrogate mother of a bird, particularly when I had a two-week European vacation coming up. I still felt a certain amount of responsibility.

That same afternoon, my son Mike and I were walking across the front yard when his size-twelve shoe narrowly missed a tiny bird on the ground. After a quick look, I realized it was the same little baby. He had hopped and fluttered about fifty feet from the pear tree. His beak was open and his wings beat passionately as he cheeped for food expressing his obvious hunger. Without doubt, the bird had been abandoned!

The only alternative was adoption. I reached down, picked up the hungry baby and carried him into the kitchen. Mike converted a cardboard box into a temporary nursery. We lined it with newspaper and placed a quart-size Mason jar filled with warm water inside to keep him from getting cold. I introduced the bird gently to his new home. While I tried to quiet the hungry fledgling, Mike busily searched the yard for suitable food. In a short time, he returned with a collection of beetles and earthworms.

Feeding the tiny bird was an interesting experience. I placed each bug or worm in his beak and poked it to the back of his throat with my little finger. That method simulated parental feeding. Young birds have difficulty swallowing food if it is not placed far enough back in their beaks. This is why baby birds appear to be pointing at the sky while receiving food. In between bits of solid food, we gave the bird a tiny amount of water from a medicine dropper. Each time my hand approached, there were excited chirps, fluttering wings and a large open bill demanding more food. He repeated this routine until he was crammed with worms and insects.

The baby slowly closed his eyes after finishing the first meal provided by his foster parents. Although I tiptoed about the kitchen, his nap lasted only a short time. Then I remembered there was a fluffy cloth in the closet. I draped it over the jar and watched as he snuggled under his soft warm blanket.

He was constantly hungry. Each time we approached the nursery, his head appeared from under the cloth with demanding chirps and open beak. If we ignored him the chirps became louder and more piercing. Locating food and responding to a demand feeding schedule gave me a better understanding of bird parenthood.

My love of birds and whatever I know about them, came from my father, who was a great naturalist and teacher. He and I spent many happy hours together as we explored all over the farm I grew up on in southern Virginia. As we strolled through field and forest and alongside streams, he paused to point out all types of plants and wildlife.

For watching small animals and other creatures, my father always chose a spot with thick cover to conceal our presence. There we sat quietly listening and observing birds and animals as he identified each species. These hikes were made more interesting by his accounts of traits unique to each creature. These experiences enriched my life and, I hope, contributed to the well-being and protection of all creatures.

My store of information on wildlife and my experience of hand-raising goslings, peachicks, guineas and ducklings gave me the confidence I needed in caring for this little baby. He demanded the necessities of life: food, water and a little companionship. Otherwise, he had few requirements.

Each day, there were remarkable changes in his development. At the end of the second week, his growth was evidence of the loving care he was receiving from his new parents. Grayish-blue pinfeathers replaced the fuzzy down and his flight feathers showed a tinge of blue. The new plumage enabled me to correctly identify the bird. He was a fledgling blue jay.

The blue jay is known to the scientific community as Cyanocitta cristata, a subspecies of the Corvidae family, which includes crows, jays, ravens and magpies. There are fifteen species that breed in North America. The jays and magpies are colorful, while crows and ravens are an iridescent black. In the Corvidae family it is difficult to distinguish male from female because they are either alike or similar in color. These birds eat a wide variety of foods, including insects, meat, fruits and grains. In fact, it has been my observation that they will eat almost anything. Blue jays that come to my feeders are especially fond of suet in the winter. This family of birds can hardly be classed as having a musical voice; most of the time it is a harsh and noisy call.

The blue jay is a beautiful bright blue bird; blue plumage on the back, wings and tail and a whitish color on the breast with a blue crest. They are fairly large birds measuring eleven to twelve inches in length when fully grown. The voice is a harsh "jeeah" or "jay jay," plus numerous other notes that can be musical and pleasing to the ear. I have also heard them imitate crows and hawks in our area. They range from the Gulf of St. Lawrence and North Manitoba to South Florida and the Gulf of

Mexico. There is some migration; when the weather becomes quite cold, they have a tendency to head a little south.

Years ago, I observed that the blue jay prefers to locate its nest in fairly tall trees. Its preference seems to be for hemlock, cedar, oak, maple, pine and spruce. It builds the nest ten to twenty feet up, usually in a crotch. The large, disorderly nest is made of a collection of sticks and grasses. The inside is a deep, smoothly-lined bowl of soft grass.

In a well-concealed nest, the female lays four to six brown-spotted, greenish eggs. The nesting female will sit in the bowl with only her head and tail showing above the top of the nest, making her almost invisible. Twelve to fourteen days after she lays the last egg, the babies begin to hatch. Their development is extremely fast and the young are able to fly in a couple of weeks. Rapid growth and fledging probably help protect them from predatory animals, including snakes and other birds.

Young jays just leaving the nest have wobbly, spindle-legs. Their wing feathers are about half-grown and their tail feathers are about an inch long. Even though the babies have left the nest, the parents continue supplying them with food as well as watching for predators.

Dull-colored plumage also helps the young, inexperienced fledgling to escape predatory animals and other birds. In fact, they are camouflaged so well that it is difficult to find a motionless baby crouching in the surrounding grass and plants. The down is totally covered by a layer of contoured feathers, which might be compared to our raincoat.

Feathers also make it possible for birds to quickly flee from predators, which are often left with a mouthful of feathers instead of a meal. The birds fluff up their plumage when threatened with danger. This ploy sometimes enables them to avoid attacks because they look twice their normal size. I have observed peafowl and guineas using the same defense when they were nesting or had a clutch of young.

At the end of two weeks, the little jay was developing a strong bond with his foster parents and was showing a great personality that rapidly won our hearts. At this point we decided that he deserved a name. The jay, after all, had survived.

With considerable time and thought, we chose to name him Mr. Jay Jay. It was a dignified name and seemed to be quite fitting.

At the tender age of three weeks, he was allowed out of the nursery box more frequently for exercise. The kitchen provided ample space for him to hop about and flap his wings. It was amusing to watch his surprise when the beating of his wings briefly lifted him off the floor. His real moment of excitement came when he fluttered his wings, gained altitude, and landed on top of the kitchen door. To us it was like seeing a child taking that first step. Learning to fly was real progress. He now held the key to freedom in his wings!

On June 14, I departed for a vacation in Europe that had been planned for three months, entrusting the care of Mr. Jay Jay to my two grown children. Each time I telephoned home, Mike and his sister Fran gave me a very descriptive report of the bird's progress. Much to my surprise, I was told they had introduced him to fresh corn, scrambled eggs and fruit, and taught him to drink water from a bowl. The thought occurred to me that my adult children were becoming bored with babysitting a bird and were teaching him to fend for himself. As the vacation clock ticked down, my desire for home, family and Mr. Jay Jay increased by the hour. After a long flight from Munich, my children met me in Ashland, Virginia. Arriving home late, I was travel weary and ready for sleep. I tiptoed into the bedroom so I didn't disturb the jay's rest. Only a flick of his wings acknowledged my presence and greetings were postponed until morning.

Dawn soon arrived and I discovered that sunrise was the signal for him to begin wake-up calls. This was accomplished by a string of "Jaeeh" shrieks, as he visited each bedroom making sure he had missed no one! He first tried to awaken each sleeper by pecking an exposed hand. If this failed, next came a gentle peck on the head that was certain to get the sleeper's attention. With his wake-up calls completed, it was back to the kitchen.

Over the two weeks I was away, there had been a notable change in Mr. Jay Jay. He was now a fat, spry juvenile with a coat of steel-blue, black and white feathers. His stubby little tail needed a bit more length, but he proudly displayed a beautiful grayish-blue crest. His tiny black eyes looked like little glass beads. He had discovered that a person's shoulder was a marvelous moving perch that provided free transportation. He had also learned to whistle and squawk and appeared to be really proud of his vocal capabilities.

The jay soon learned that his different calls and actions brought different results. When we began serving dinner his "Jaeeh" was in a softer voice and then his plate was placed on the table. He announced his bedtime hour with a couple of shrieks as he headed for the door in the den and waited until I turned on the light in the bedroom. As soon as he wanted to go outside in the morning he sounded off with a string of loud "Jaeehs" sending me to open the door.

Because he had known only affection and tenderness in his life, he was in no way afraid of humans at this age. Mr. Jay Jay later became distrustful or perhaps jealous of strangers but even then he didn't display any fear of people. He developed a liking for companionship at an early

"Look what I found!"

age. There was no doubt that the jay enjoyed being with family members because he was quite sociable in our presence.

Mr. Jay Jay promptly learned the routine of the household. Early in the morning he proceeded from alarm clock duty to the kitchen patrol, using the top of the door for his lookout post. This vantage point provided him with a great view of the entire kitchen. As soon as I opened the refrigerator door, he flew inside, walking on the shelves or anything else that happened to be in his path while he sampled any food within his reach. He next discovered the egg tray and in a second cracked an egg and drank the contents. His fondness for eggs may have been an inherited trait, unique to that species. Different types of birds have different food requirements. Some eat seeds, fruits, insects or a combination of these foods. I have noted that jays and crows do sometimes visit other bird's nests and steal eggs. It came as no surprise that he preferred the kitchen, because here he usually found food and family.

About a week after I returned home, I decided that it was necessary for Mr. Jay Jay to be outdoors again. To keep this wild bird in captivity had never been my plan. He had received the physical relief he needed; the time had come to reintroduce him to his original world. He was healthy, completely feathered, very intelligent, and capable of surviving in nature's environment.

A little background about our family is in order here, I think. My husband and I were married in June 1951 and two years later decided to pursue the nursery business. We purchased a 50 acre farm in Louisa County, Virginia. During the fifties our two children were born and in the spring of 1959 we added a greenhouse to our operation, growing vegetable and flower plants. When our customers began to ask for floral arrangements we realized there was no florist in the county and converted our home basement to a shop that we moved to adjoin one of the greenhouses five years later. Sadly, my husband died in 1967, leaving me a widow who never remarried. The children and I decided to remain on the farm, continuing the business operation, with which they helped tremendously until they left for college in the early seventies. In

1974 I relocated the shop to a shopping center in the town of Louisa to which I drove to work every day. June 1979 was when Mr. Jay Jay fell into our lives. Mike was 26 and Fran was 23. With our combined efforts the business was very successful, achieving goals that surpassed my expectations.

Our farm was an ideal habitat, capable of providing food and cover for the jay. Just beyond the yard were open fields, 20 acres of beautiful woods, and a sparkling pond. It had always been a wildlife sanctuary, especially dedicated to birds. Having evaluated the situation, I proceeded with my plan for releasing the jay.

On the morning of June 30, Mr. Jay Jay, being unaware of the plan for the day, enjoyed his usual breakfast with the family. His white plate was served with scrambled eggs, bread, and a ripe juicy strawberry. When he had finished his serving, he flew to everyone's shoulder begging for an extra helping. If we didn't share our food with him, he would wait for a chance to steal a bit from our plates. He then carried the extra pieces to various rooms, stuffing them under pillows, in the sofa, chair or in my purse for future use. The more I observed the jay, the more convinced I became that he could fend for himself.

June 30 marked five weeks since his rescue. It was also the date that I chose to reintroduce him into the wild. After breakfast, I walked out onto the back patio with him perched on my shoulder. He sat very still and quiet, while he observed his surroundings. As Mr. Jay Jay stepped onto my hand, I gently placed him on the back of a chaise longue. Within a few minutes he turned his eyes toward the sky and began singing with joy. He seemed to be saying, "Hey, this isn't really bad—I don't see any walls." Since he was accustomed to the confines of the house, the wide-open space appeared to be a momentary puzzle.

I then went into the house so that I could watch his activity while he was unaware of my presence. In fifteen or twenty minutes he gained enough courage to take off on his first flight. He drifted down and settled into a viburnum bush near the corner of the patio, about fifteen feet from the chaise. From this point Mr. Jay Jay flew to a nearby pear tree,

Reintroduction to his outside world

where he had his first encounter with an unfriendly mockingbird. He quickly decided it was time to look for another area and headed toward the woods behind the house. My eyes could not follow his rapid flight and I lost sight of him.

When I had finished the morning chores, I went out and worked in the rock garden until lunch. I listened for the jay as I pulled up weeds and pruned spent perennials, occasionally whistling and calling to him. He had usually responded to my whistle inside either by flying to me or giving a series of "Jaeeh" calls. This time, I heard no answer.

Then, in mid-afternoon, I heard a raucous jay voice coming from the back yard. There he was, sitting in the pear tree. Thinking he might be hungry and thirsty on a hot day, I filled his white dish with water, rushed outside, and held it in the palm of my hand. Instantly he flew down for a drink and a bath. My clothes were damp after he finished his bath, but the pleasure of watching him made it worthwhile. Food appeared to be secondary; evidently he had found all the insects he needed for lunch. After satisfying his thirst and drying his feathers he sailed off toward the woods.

Six o'clock came and the jay had not been heard from since lunch. During dinner, we talked mainly about his absence. We began to wonder if he would come back home at night. The only leftover from our dinner was the food on the jay's plate.

After washing the dishes and tidying up the kitchen, we went outside to enjoy the cool evening breeze and listen for Mr. Jay Jay. With dusk approaching, Mike and Fran began calling him. All of a sudden, we heard a "Jeeah" squawk and fluttering wings. It was the jay, headed straight for the house, hovering in mid-air until I opened the door. Oh, what excitement! He seemed to be saying, "I'm home. Let me in." When he glided inside, he caught sight of his food dish. The jay landed on the back of the chair and hopped onto the table, and began to eat hungrily. After stuffing himself, he flew to the curtain rod to wipe his beak and spruce up.

When bedtime arrived, he squawked and hurried to my bedroom. The jay sailed up to his usual night time spot, the cornice over the window, tucked his head under his wing and promptly went to sleep. He chose this location as a night roost after he had tried unsuccessfully to perch on several pictures on the wall. It was the highest point in the room and I could only imagine that his choice was instinctive. The height apparently gave him a sense of security.

I must admit that I was elated that Mr. Jay Jay was safe and sound after his first excursion, but I had really never thought he would return home for the night-time. As the days passed, however, we had fallen in love with this little guy. After he had refused my first invitation to leave and join his own kind, I opened the house and put out the welcome mat. No room was off limits. I was reconciled to sharing my worldly possessions with my feathered friend.

It began to appear possible that Mr. Jay Jay would continue to live in our house. But not wanting my house to resemble an aviary, I devised a method of maintaining tidiness. After determining his favorite perching spots, it was a fairly simple matter to cover the area with plastic film. Mr. Jay Jay had impeccable bathroom habits. I cannot remember a single time when he soiled my clothing while sitting on my shoulder.

The next morning after breakfast, the jay and I again ventured outdoors. This time there was no hesitation; he flew swiftly to the woods. During the day he made occasional trips back to the yard.

Mr. Jay Jay developed a daily pattern of eating breakfast with the family, asking me to open the door to his first world and coming home at night to his second world.

There was one remaining problem: my florist shop located in a nearby town, kept me away from home all day six days a week. I realized that the jay needed access to the house during my absence. Leaving the kitchen window open five inches was the answer. This allowed him to be a totally independent bird, free to come and go at will.

The ball of down which I had rescued two months before had developed into a beautiful, healthy jay. Hand-rearing the orphan had been successful and his devotion was my reward. But my responsibility did not end there.

I had simply given the jay an early chance at survival. Much was still needed if I was to reintroduce him into his natural world. I was committed to this plan. Each new day brought with it a challenge and the anticipation of a fascinating new experience.

If you've noticed that I haven't mentioned our strong shepherd, Heidi, who had so gently nudged Mr. Jay Jay into our lives, it's not because I have forgotten her. Sadly, she met with a not so gentle end while I was away in Europe. Fran had bought this lovely dog only a month before my trip. In a bizarre twist, while I was in Switzerland visiting the Heidi Memorial, she was killed in a highway accident.

Chapter Two

Escapades

Mr. Jay Jay soon learned that the window was always open during the daytime. A lamp bracket above the table held his water bowl. A small plate was filled each morning with his favorite foods and left on the table or in the window. This arrangement furnished the jay with all the comforts of home while I was away from the house. There was only one minor problem. When he vigorously bathed himself, he often soaked the surrounding area. But little time was required to tidy up after the jay and that was a small price to pay for the delight and amusement he provided.

During the day, Mr. Jay Jay spent most of his time

away from the house making only an occasional trip back to the yard. I was generally home around 5:00 P.M. and it became obvious that he was aware of my schedule. When I got back from work I would find him already inside the house waiting for me. He would be sitting in the dining room window waiting to catch a glimpse of my car. From there he had an unobstructed view of the driveway and parking area. He seemed to recognize our family vehicles and I could count on hearing his distinctive voice as I drove into my parking space. As soon as I opened the door, he left his window spot and flew to me with a cheerful greeting. The delight he displayed for returning family members was always a moving experience.

On weekend mornings, Mr. Jay Jay was not always successful in bringing life to the family's sleeping bodies. Breakfast was usually served later than on the weekdays, but the jay kept to his own schedule. After failing to rouse us, he would fly to the kitchen in search of any visible food. He was not too choosy on those occasions, and all accessible fruits were in jeopardy—tomatoes, peaches, and apples—anything he could find.

When the jay couldn't find any food in the kitchen, he resorted to his secret pantry—the underside of rugs and pillows and in other crevices that he had well stocked with bits of food. Jays are notorious hoarders of food and very secretive about hiding it. We laughed at the caution he used when retrieving hidden goodies. If surprised by an intruder, he went into a state of suspended animation, standing stock still until the individual left. When he felt the coast was clear, he would retrieve the food and return to the kitchen with his dry tidbit, which he then soaked in his water dish before eating.

Summer arrived and so did the Japanese beetles. Now, gardeners hate these destructive insects, but we quickly found that blue jays love them. We often offered them to him as a reward for the comical tricks he performed. A jelly jar was used for collecting and storing the insects. It was the ideal container, because Mr. Jay Jay could easily see how many beetles were stored for his pleasure. When he performed a trick for us, the jar top was removed and the jay was allowed to pick out a juicy beetle. Fran used this ploy so she could watch him swoop and glide through the air. She would catch a grasshopper, and while holding it in mid-air he would dive in at great speed plucking it from her fingers. When he became tired of this game, he alighted on top of her head for a brief rest.

Whenever the family was present, the jay went into his "performer" mode. He was fascinated with pens, pencils and anything else small enough for him to remove from a tabletop or a shirt pocket. He did not like cigarettes and took personal offense when they were left out on a counter or table. He would extract a cigarette from the pack and then proceed to attack it until it was thoroughly shredded. Perhaps Mr. Jay Jay knew they were not edible because of the odor. My daughter Fran and I were the smokers in the family but Mr. Jay Jay never scolded us for our evil ways.

Curiosity was one of his dominant traits. He was enchanted with ice trays just removed from the refrigerator. The jay walked around with his head cocked to the side while he looked at the tray

"Destroy these things!"

from all angles. After thoroughly checking it out, he first tested it with his beak and then attacked it with rapid pecks like an ice pick. He would pick up a piece of ice and hold it for a few seconds, repeating this process until the tray was removed, the contents melted or the cubes were reduced to chips. Whether he was fascinated or bewildered by the cold, sparkling cubes we never figured out.

Toward the end of July, I began to hear shrieking jays as they passed over the yard heading for the tall trees near the pond. My young jay was excited by this noisy group of birds. Their loud "Jaeeh, Jaeeh" sounds reminded me of an old saying that after you first hear the sounds of jays, the first frost is only ninety days away. Our family jay played with the newcomers all day and then returned to spend the night with us. I wondered what would happen when our yard jays made their migration a little south.

On the first of August, when I returned home from work Mr. Jay Jay was nowhere to be found. At first I thought he might be taking a late play day, but as we finished dinner with night approaching, he still hadn't shown up. We went outside to look for him, calling, whistling and shouting until darkness fell, all without an answering "Jaeeh." We went to bed feeling sure he would show up for breakfast with the family. Morning came, though, and all the jays seemed to have vanished.

I went to work as usual and returned home fully expecting Mr. Jay Jay to greet me, but again there was no sign of him. I clung to the hope of seeing him, but when the third day passed, I began to think he wasn't going to return.

A couple of years earlier, my son had discovered a plucking post in the woods behind the house. This is a spot used by hawks to kill and pluck their prey, and is usually littered with feathers from songbirds and jays. Not only had I seen red tail hawks and crows flying over the area, but I had also seen a hawk sitting in the walnut tree in the back yard. Hawks sometimes come to an area with bird feeders looking for song birds that are easy prey. I had a glimmer of fear that this might have been the fate of my jay. At the end of the fifth day, I had really begun to give up hope of his return. I missed the cheerful "Jaeeh Jaeeh" welcome home and we all missed his entertaining and playful mischief.

That evening I was cooking dinner, when all of a sudden I heard Mr. Jay Jay at the window, which was closed in his absence. Frantically beating his wings, he seemed to be saying, "Hurry up and, open the window!" As I raised the window he scuttled inside and with a quick hop made it to the dinner table. He was ready for dinner and appeared to be as excited as we were about the family reunion.

Many years later, I learned from a neighbor the reason for his five-day absence. The jay had flown to a neighborhood a mile or so away from our farm. He chose a particular house and perched in a nearby tree with his eyes fixed on the entrance, waiting for the door to open. When the lady of the house stepped out on the porch, Mr. Jay Jay flew to her shoulder taking her completely by surprise. She shooed him from her shoulder and began to duck back into the house, but as she opened the door he darted inside ahead of her.

Because of the bird's arrival and strange, to her, behavior, she thought him to be a bird of ill omen. At that time, her mother was critically ill, and over the years she had heard tales of birds being the bearer of a death notice. A little more study on folklore, and she would have learned that most birds of ill omen are supposed to be black, not bright blue.

Mr. Jay Jay made himself comfortable in her house and she did provide some bread for him, which must have seemed to him like an invitation to enjoy her hospitality. As he explored the interior of her house, he must have soon discovered that there were no open doors or windows. Alas, he had flown into a trap! The lady of the house was equally concerned, as she was trying to figure how to catch the bird and remove it from her home. All she had to do was open a door or window, but that didn't occur to her right away. By the fifth day, they both must have been tired of each other's forced company and the lady was finally inspired to just leave the door open and hope for the best.

The pet jay didn't need a better invitation to leave, and he sailed out her door and flew home. After his noisy arrival and demand for entrance, he was obviously delighted to be home again. The evening meal was one of his favorite times, but that night he was unusually lively, even helping clean the plates by tucking food scraps into the folds of the dishtowel. After dinner, he performed a home inspection, flying from room to room, alighting at his old hangouts and looking into all his secret places to check on his stash of food and toys.

He retired for the evening in his special nook above my bedroom window, and awoke the next morning as daybreak began to peek through the window. I couldn't be certain whether it was the pale light of dawn or the stirring of a peafowl in an oak tree outside the bedroom that aroused him. A regular morning feature was the fluttering of peafowl wings as they descended to the ground from roosting in an oak tree. I could see Mr. Jay Jay welcome the dawning day as he stretched his wings and legs, before swishing out of the bedroom for the kitchen.

Later, when I entered the kitchen, I found him taking his morning bath. He was standing in his water dish splashing around and energetically flapping his wings, thoroughly soaking the tablecloth. The world seemed right again with Mr. Jay Jay home and

An insect game with Fran

Helping with cleanup detail

"This truck really needs work."

Mr. Jay Jay's morning bath

Beating the August heat and inspecting the crop

"Whew, sleep is great."

Good-bye to Mike

Mr. Jay Jay and Miss Jay at feeder January 14

I proceeded to prepare his breakfast of chopped fruit and scrambled eggs. When he finished eating I opened the storm door and when he heard it squeak, he shot through it for another day of jay play.

Apparently his vacation had not altered his daily habits, whatever they were. I had often wondered how the jay occupied his daylight hours. I could picture him soaring over fields and woods in search of insects, or a mate, or just quietly sitting on a limb enjoying the beauty of nature. With his in-house food program, our jay did not have the food urgency of his fellow jays. He seemed to be staying closer to home now, and the next two weeks passed in a fairly normal fashion.

Mr. Jay Jay's uncanny perception of human action never ceased to amaze me. Often he appeared to know my plans before they were executed. It was as if he were reading my mind and, as before, I was disappointed that we could not communicate with each other in the same language.

Shortly after his return, the children and I decided to take a short day trip. The day began with the usual routine. We had breakfast with Mr. Jay

Jay, and as soon as the door opened he flew swiftly to his daytime activities.

Before long, we left the house and headed for the station wagon parked in the front driveway. When I opened the car door, a blue missile appeared out of nowhere, landed on the open door and then fluttered down to the floorboard. From there he flew to the ash tray. With his neck stretched out, and peering up, he seemed to be asking, "What are you waiting for, let's go." It was quite plain that he expected to be included in this Sunday outing. His next move was to fly to the steering wheel, gripping it with all of his toes, ready to assist with the driving.

We tried to shoo him out of the car but, by his body language and raised crest, he informed us that he was not intimidated and didn't plan to move an inch. Trying to explain why a trip to the city was not appropriate for a "country bird" was unsuccessful. Finally we all exited the car, as if the trip was off, and coaxed him out with a cookie. Then we jumped back into the car and made a rapid takeoff for our trip. As we sped down the lane, he hurried to a crabapple tree for a quick glimpse, expressing his anger and disappointment with ear- piercing shrieks.

After a pleasant day, we returned home sure that Mr. Jay Jay had forgotten the trickery that removed him from the car. We were wrong. We pulled up in front of the house and instead of his standard welcoming and alighting on my shoulder he soared to the top of a tree and greeted us with a loud "Jaeeh" sound in a distinctly scolding tone. When we opened the door, he flew past us straight to his dinner bowl. As soon as he finished eating, he quickly retired to his night roost, ignoring us for the rest of the day like a pouting child.

As time passed, the jay became our security system, a self- appointed house guard. Not only did he have incredible hearing, but he also could distinguish one automobile from another, by its sound. He recognized the sound of our vehicles, station wagon, van, dump truck and tractor, and never raised an alarm as they traveled up and down the driveway. If a strange vehicle approached the house, he would suddenly make a noisy appearance, circle the area and then fly to the peak of the roof for a better look.

The minute the door of an unknown car was opened, he was again in the sky doing close surveillance. When the visitor moved toward the house, our jay provided escort service by flying abreast or hovering above the person's head. This usually resulted in a wary approach by any visitors, giving us enough time to come out and greet them, at which point Mr. Jay Jay retired from the scene.

He generally accepted women visitors but was frequently hostile toward men. Whenever my pet attacked someone, I tried to figure out his motive. He didn't hesitate to screech a warning when I was approached, and if the warning was unheeded, he would attack. We have all heard about the protective instinct of mothers in the wild, and apparently it also applies to offspring toward their adoptive mothers. This innate sense of "belonging" may have been manifested as jealousy or as a protective reaction. At less than four months, my little male adoptee had become very protective of me. This trait may have been due to instinct or imprinting.

Imprinting is learning that occurs rapidly and

very early in life. Birds and animals imprint on the person who has supplied them with food while they are very young. The jay was about two weeks old when we found him. He became used to seeing a human face and imprinted with humans instead of birds. This was my explanation for the jay's unusual behavior.

One day, a gentleman approached the house while ignoring the jay's security measures. As the man neared the front door, Mr. Jay Jay swooped down and raked his feet through the man's hair. We intervened, saving our visitor from any more attacks.

Then there was the "observe and attack" incident. A neighbor came to inquire about borrowing a tractor. As the man began his walk up the brick path between two oak trees, the jay came on the scene. The moment the man's feet touched the patio, our self-appointed security guard aggressively attacked him. Needless to say, it was the man's first experience with a hostile bird. He bolted to the door and made it into the living room. The jay was still on guard duty and sneaked through the kitchen window, announced his presence with a raucous squawk and flew into the living room, where he continued his watch from the curtain rod.

Toward the end of summer, Mike decided it was time to overhaul the old dump truck. First he moved it to the side yard where it would be easier to take out the old worn-out engine and install a new one. Moving the truck and Mike's activity at the new site quickly attracted the attention of the always inquisitive Mr. Jay Jay. Being a responsible bird, our jay gave up his free-flying day excursions for close supervision of the truck repair. He perched sometimes on the truck roof, sometimes on the window frame and sometimes on the steering wheel, unless he wanted the full bird's eye view from an overhanging oak tree. The repair project neared completion and when Mike jumped into the driver's seat to fire up the engine, Mr. Jay Jay joined him, perching on the steering wheel. Both of them seemed eager to turn the key and hear the purring of the engine. The engine started with loud sputtering and backfiring, none of which fazed the jay, who wasn't afraid of loud noises. After a small adjustment to the carburetor, the noise abated and Mike was ready for a road test. The jay flew alongside the truck as it rumbled down the lane. With the successful overhaul, we declared the bird a first-class mechanic.

Having successfully supervised the engine repair, Mr. Jay Jay evidently thought he needed some playtime. When the test drive was completed, he flew off to the woods. He was neither seen nor heard from for the rest of the day.

That evening, the jay was home in time for dinner and then entertained us with what he had learned during his afternoon of play. He flew to the top of the door and uncharacteristically began preening his tousled feathers. All at once, he started bobbing his head up and down, accompanied by an unusual vocal sound. Mimicry is a common characteristic of blue jays, and while I knew he was mimicking something, it took a while for me to identify the sound he was working on. He kept practicing, until I recognized that he was imitating a crow, a sound that became a permanent part of his vocabulary.

Summer in Virginia was always a busy and joyful time for me, and a vegetable garden was part of the summer ritual. Preparing the ground and planting was followed by what seemed a never-ending task of pulling weeds. This summer was more joyful than most, because Mr. Jay Jay was my frequent companion. As I cultivated around the plants, he stayed nearby hunting insects or just resting on my shoulder. It was funny to watch him ferret out the pesky insects. He hopped along the rows occasionally pausing to listen and peer underneath the plants. The second he spotted the prey, there was a flutter of wings as he pounced on the bug.

Mr. Jay Jay was quite fastidious about what he liked. His taste buds were extremely selective. The jay's favorite farm-fresh tidbit was the grasshopper, an insect that was always abundant in our garden. He did not like stink bugs at all.

With the garden, came the gathering of the crop and a new amusement for Mr. Jay Jay. After harvesting the vegetables I carried them into the kitchen to wash them in the large sink. Turning on the faucet caught our jay's attention and he watched intently while the sink filled with water. When I looked up and saw his twitching wings, I immediately knew his intentions. The sound of running water inspired him to take a bath. With his crest erect, he flew to the sink, and settled on the floating mustard greens. When the greens began to sink under his weight, he found himself breast deep in water. By strenuously beating his wings, the wet jay was able to climb out of the sink. He hopped onto the cabinet, briskly shaking his body to rid his feathers of the excess water. He then flew to the top of the refrigerator and began preening his soggy plumage.

He apparently thought the bath in mustard greens had been a fortunate accident, because in a few days he was again at the sink. I ran several inches of water in the sink and let the faucet continue to drip. The jay jumped into the water and gave signs of pure enjoyment as he frolicked in his newfound bathtub. He had plainly outgrown his white dish.

His intelligence continued to surprise me. As I walked through fields and woods on the farm, the jay always seemed to know where I was. When blackberries and huckleberries began to ripen, I collected my baskets and went in search of them. These berries were highly prized for making wine and jelly. A short time after I had located a productive patch, I heard my pet "Jeeah" as he headed for a landing on my head. After checking out the contents of my basket, he hopped down and sat on the handle for easy access to the already picked berries. This bird was no dummy and quickly figured out that it was easier to get berries from my basket than from a thorny bush.

Obviously the jay had no plans for remaining outdoors during the night; his preference was my bedroom. I really didn't want him to roost on the cornice and I resolved that problem by installing a curtain rod that was the correct size for his feet, midway in the window. Because I enjoyed his companionship as much as he seemed to enjoy mine, I didn't banish him from my room.

Occasionally my bedtime came earlier than his. When this happened, I simply said, "Jay Jay, get on your perch. It's bedtime." The amazing thing was that he appeared to understand this command. He would immediately fly to the rod, fluff his feathers and pull up one foot indicating he was ready for sleep.

As August drew to an end, I returned home one evening and did not receive any greeting from Mr. Jay Jay. Remembering his earlier mini-vacation, I didn't become too concerned this time. It was also possible that he had outgrown his adopted family and now wanted to join his own kind. It is human nature to become attached to a pet and as the second day of his absence ended, I wondered where the jay could be.

Sunday, day three of his absence, came and I occupied myself with house cleaning, followed by cooking. I decided to bake a cake and as I measured out the ingredients I heard a familiar jay voice and the scrape of bird toenails on the sill. Looking toward the window, I saw Mr. Jay Jay bobbing his head up and down and pecking at the glass.

As soon as he tumbled inside, I knew there was a problem. He sagged down on the table with one wing hanging low, and he was obviously in pain. I picked him up, examined the injured wing and determined it was not broken, just badly sprained. He didn't seem capable of flying so I placed him on the kitchen curtain rod. He tucked his head under his good wing and drifted off to sleep.

Dinnertime came and I gave him a painless ride on my hand to the table. To make him feel better, I served his plate with a variety of his favorite foods. Without any enthusiasm, he ate only a small amount and then tried to fly to the door. He didn't have the strength and crash landed on the floor. Before I could reach him, he made a second take-off attempt and again fluttered to the floor. He then hopped toward me with a pathetic look, as if asking me for help. Mr. Jay Jay climbed on my arm and snuggled to my body with a soft "Jaeeh, Jaeeh," in the manner of a thank you instead of a plea for help. After I had consoled him for a while, I placed him on his perch for a restful night.

As the first streaks of light announced another day, the jay stretched his limbs. Apparently he had forgotten about his injury, because I could see his surprise when he tried to flex his stiff wing. Being grounded is usually a death sentence for a bird, and although Mr. Jay Jay was safe, it was still a terrible predicament. Realizing he couldn't fly, he voiced three "Jaeeh" calls, obviously asking for assistance. I moved him from the bedroom perch to the kitchen window where he could look outside. I could imagine how he yearned to be outdoors, but until his wing healed, he was housebound.

I never found out for certain what injured him. But during this period he seemed bedeviled by the sound of crows in the nearby woods. Having mastered the art of mimicking crows, he now began to answer their calls as if he wanted them to think he was one of them. His reaction to the sound of crows led me to believe he had been in a brawl with them and had come out the loser.

Although Mr. Jay Jay was bored with his flightless life, that was his fate until he fully recovered from his injury. As the pain and swelling lessened, he began exercising by traveling everywhere on foot. Each day he showed remarkable improvement and by the end of the week he was flapping his wings in pure delight.

He now reacted with a look of anticipation

each time he heard the jiggle of the back-door latch. To test his readiness for flight, he began to flit through the house, using his feet to bounce off the walls. That performance convinced me that he had returned to good health and was ready for the outdoors. I pushed open the kitchen door and he flew out letting loose a couple of "Jaeeh, Jaeeh's" announcing to the world that he was back in the sky.

Chapter Three

Summer Finale

The soft, haunting songs of fall warblers and the chirping katydids in the evening reminded me that summer was slipping away. The jays outdoors were very vocal, apparently sensing the approaching change of seasons. Each morning after Mr. Jay Jay heard the alluring calls of other blue jays in the woods, he waited eagerly for the door to open. However, when something captured his interest inside he would stay in with the people. That did not always work to his advantage.

I had bought a nice batch of fiery red-chili peppers from a local produce stand. I planned to use them in pickled dilly beans and hot pepper jelly.

The remainders of the peppers were to be strung and dried for later enjoyment as seasoning and decorations. While I located a sharp needle, thread and gloves in preparation for stringing chilies, Mr. Jay Jay put in an appearance. Being interested in what I was doing, he was in no hurry to leave and play with his buddies. The string of red peppers fascinated him as I threaded them through the stems. While I worked, I wondered how long it would be before he became an active participant.

A few minutes later, my pet hopped over, snatched a pepper from the basket, and flew to the top of the door with it in his beak. The jay's feet had barely touched the door when he voiced a loud squawk and dropped the chili. He raked his beak back and forth on the door and then hurried to his water bowl. After trying to quench the fire in his beak, he sailed out the window and headed toward the woods. This was one pretty vegetable Mr. Jay Jay didn't want to sample again.

The last two weeks of August that year were extremely busy on the farm, especially in the greenhouses. Thousands of poinsettia cuttings waited to be placed in pots, and the preparation of the soil required a considerable amount of effort. After the soil was mixed, the wagon was pulled into position alongside the large sliding door. The stacked pots and young plants were placed within easy reach of the employees so they could be quickly filled with soil and plants potted. Then the plants were carried into the greenhouse and placed on benches under mist. Mr. Jay Jay was always ready to lend a helping beak. He was constantly in the middle of the action, either sitting on the wagon or on the pile of soil. Searching for small pebbles gave him a full-time job. A shiny bit of stone entertained him for five or ten minutes, while he picked it up and dropped it into a pot or poked it into another spot in the pile of soil. Wherever there was action, the jay was sure to be found.

The greenhouse was equipped with an automatic mist system that operated at fifteen-minute intervals. Another nice feature was the "fan and pad" air-conditioning unit. In a very short time the jay discovered the comfort of the greenhouse and its special features.

Each day in mid-afternoon, the jay appeared in the greenhouse, walking up and down the benches as if inspecting the crop. It was a great place to escape the layers of impenetrable August heat. It was quite cool and damp with abundant plant life, resembling a tropical rain forest.

As soon as the mist system was activated, Mr. Jay Jay began to show off. He bobbed merrily from side to side with his head thrust forward, while vigorously fluttering his wings. My Jay Jay had just discovered the delights of his own personal automated bathing facility.

During the hot, sunny days of August, I would often go to the garden to see if the rosemary, marjoram and basil were ready to be harvested and dried for winter use. Herbs contain more concentrated oil when picked during the hottest part of the day. Mr. Jay Jay rode along on my shoulder as I gathered and filled the basket with each of these aromatic herbs, which would then be air-dried and preserved for future use in cooking and in potpourris. The next chore was to rinse them until they were clean and then place them on paper towels to drain. That wasn't good enough for Mr. Jay Jay, however. He hopped over to the pile of greenery, cocked his head to the side for a better view and pulled a bug from beneath a leaf. Thanks to Mr. Jay Jay's help the herbs were not only free of dust, but free of insects too.

As helpful as he was, he sometimes seemed to have a vengeful bent. One morning the jay left his night roost ahead of schedule. He seemed to have something quite important on his mind. When I entered the kitchen, he sailed over to the outside door with a loud "Jaeeh" which was a little out of character, since he usually wanted breakfast first. But instead of opening that door, I opened the refrigerator door. The instant he saw the refrigerator door open he flew straight for the egg tray and rapidly pecked holes in five eggs. I suppose he had been annoyed when I ignored his first request to go outdoors and felt this was a justified method of revenge. There were a number of other occasions when he was quite a mischief-maker. When I flipped the dish towel toward him, he jeered at me, and I perceived a glint of devilment in his eye as he hurried to the window.

As soon as we finished breakfast, I opened the door and Mr. Jay Jay hurried outside. My chore for the morning was to complete the last step of a recipe for watermelon-rind pickle. My family didn't think the pantry was well stocked without that delectable treat. While the vinegar and spice solution came to a rolling boil, I packed the rind into the hot jars. The house was filled with the aroma.

I had just finished sealing the last jar when the jay arrived at the window. It was lunch time! He hopped into the kitchen and immediately hopped right back outside. He then began to shake his head vigorously and wipe his beak on the window sill. One whiff of the strong vinegar and spices was all he could tolerate and, deciding that lunch was going to be better outdoors that day, he flapped back to the woods for the balance of the afternoon.

The summer days had begun to grow shorter and the crickets had begun their nocturnal chorus as they crept inside the house in search of a winter home. This was a reminder for Mike that it was time to mow the knee-high peppergrass in the fields for the last time before the cold weather arrived.

Mr. Jay Jay always appeared on the scene when he heard the tractor operating. Traveling through the tall grass, the tractor and mower flushed insects out of their hiding places. The jay hovered alongside the tractor, diving down and catching the easy prey. After following the equipment all day and stuffing himself with bugs, he was not overly excited about dinner that evening. In fact, when he came into the house, he never even paused in the kitchen, but instead went straight to bed. It had been a long, hard day and the jay was completely worn out.

The next morning was sunny and cool, a welcome relief from the previous week of scorching temperatures. Mr. Jay Jay was unusually vocal, imitating meadowlarks, crows and family whistles and answering other jays in the yard. He flew to the window with a longing look, as if to say, "Hurry up, it's a beautiful day. Let me out." In a few minutes he was out of the house and sitting in the apple tree near the kitchen. He had a mischievous swagger in his walk as he strutted back and forth on the limb, apparently listening for something. Then suddenly his crest shot up and he darted over the back field toward some tall trees. He had obviously heard something interesting.

A cooler morning was the inspiration I needed to do some pruning and weeding in the rock garden. Because of a rainy summer, the shrubs had made tremendous growth and the area began to resemble a jungle. I had always waited until the birds had finished raising their families before pruning and shaping the various flowering shrubs and evergreens. The thick foliage afforded excellent cover. In fact, the Julianne barberry, a thorny bush, was always claimed by the mockingbirds. That garden was a quiet, secluded spot that provided a perfect place to rear the fledglings. Judging from the number of empty nests and immature birds I observed, it had ended up being a successful year.

In a short time, I heard my pet "Jaeehing" as he glided toward me and landed on my shoulder. While I snipped branches in the sunny part of the garden, Mr. Jay Jay looked for bugs. Before long I noticed that he was panting and holding his wings out from his body. Being in the sunlight for a lengthy time was not his cup of tea. He quickly decided that the redbud tree was a better choice on a sunny day.

Later that afternoon, I picked up my gathering basket and headed to the vegetable garden. The dried butterbeans were ready to be harvested for use in the winter. The jay was sitting in the pear tree and by the time I set the basket down in the row, he was there to help. The beans made a rattling noise as I pulled them from the vines. Mr. Jay Jay perched on the handle of the wicker basket with an inquisitive look on his face. The strange sound seemed to bewilder him. He hopped to the ground, not knowing what to think of the peculiar noise. His crest lifted and so did his courage. He eventually walked up to a vine, pecked a pod and immediately jumped backward in the row. After pecking the pod several times, he opened it exposing the seed, which he then tried to eat. The bean was too large for him to swallow whole and too hard for him to break up.

When I had finished picking beans, it was time to think about preparing our evening meal. I grabbed the basket and hurried to the house, leaving Mr. Jay

Jay in the garden. I emptied the beans onto a piece of newspaper and began to plan the menu.

As I worked in the kitchen, I noticed there was no breeze stirring. The humid air hung oppressively over the ground. When I looked outside, I saw numerous thunderheads in the western sky. There was a distant peal of thunder, followed by rolling sounds across the heavens. The clouds gathered rapidly and the wind soon increased to the intensity of a gale. Mr. Jay Jay was not yet home.

Just as the rain began pelting the roof and walls of the house, Fran closed the kitchen window. A few seconds later, we heard the jay frantically calling. He was sitting on the sill eager to come inside and escape the storm.

Fran quickly opened the window for Mr. Jay Jay and just as quickly slammed it shut. A dreadful squawk followed. The bird's back toe had been caught in the closing window. Fortunately the toe was not broken, but it was severely bruised. It was another painful episode for the jay.

The question next was how to administer first aid to the jay's injured toe. Certainly, he was not in the mood to sit still for an ice pack treatment, but he was in great need of help. After thinking about what could be done to help him, I made a concoction of two drops of whiskey and a tiny amount of water. With a little coaxing, he slowly drank the medicine from a teaspoon. The aim was to bring sleep, thereby easing his pain.

In a few minutes, Mr. Jay Jay flew to the living room. He chose a quiet area and settled in for the night. A little later, when I checked on him, he was sound asleep on the curtain rod with the injured foot tucked up in his feathers. The remedy was evidently successful because he appeared to be unaware of any pain. Not having the heart to disturb his rest, I left him there for the night.

The next morning he was up at dawn, but lacked his usual enthusiasm. When I looked at his foot, I discovered a very swollen toe. He limped along on one foot or flew only short distances in the house. Mr. Jay Jay's appetite was somewhat diminished and he showed no interest in going outside. All that day he sat quietly with ruffled feathers, indicating his discomfort.

On the second day he showed a bit of improvement. Instead of limping on one foot, he was hopping along and was more drawn to his food dish. The lameness lasted about five days, but it was at least a week before he walked in a normal manner. In the meantime, he sat in the window and called to his buddies.

During the week that Mr. Jay Jay was housebound, he discovered some interesting gadgets. Many of my evenings at home were spent doing bookkeeping for the florist shop. For this purpose, I used an old adding machine which I kept on a small table. The jay was quite attracted to the machine, so much so that he left his perch to play with it, even though he was half asleep. While I pushed keys and pulled the handle, he stood next to my elbow watching every move.

Often when the adding machine was not in use, he would stand on the keys as if he were trying to figure out what made it function. Soon he was trying to move the handle, imitating my actions. Although he didn't have the capability to do this, he appeared to understand the principle. And we understood the principle too: Whatever a person did, he was eager to try.

At the end of his forced vacation, we were relieved to learn that he had not suffered any permanent disability from the window mishap and it didn't change his affection for the family.

Fully recovered, Mr. Jay Jay was once again ready for open skies and sunlit fields. Like him, I too found pleasure in wandering the woodland paths in search of plants and wildlife. My pet sometimes accompanied me on those walks, flying from tree to tree or riding along on my shoulder. One incident in particular that I thought amusing was the time I found a box turtle while I strolled alongside a small stream. When I reached down and picked up the critter, the jay scurried to the nearest tree with his crest standing straight up. After thinking about the situation, he drifted down to my shoulder and then attacked the turtle I was holding in my hand. I never knew whether he was frightened or was trying to protect me from what he perceived to be harmful.

Another reptile the jay disliked intensely was the black rat snake. Whenever that predator trespassed in the yard, Mr. Jay Jay joined the other birds fighting it. All the raucous "Jaeehing" and squawking was bound to bring a family member in a hurry. Mr. Jay Jay, catbirds and mockingbirds all joined in the battle diving toward the snake, fiercely pecking it in an effort to drive it away. Quite often snakes rob bird nests, swallowing the eggs or their chicks. As soon as they were satisfied that the reptile was no longer a threat, peace and quiet returned to the yard.

I was relaxing in the kitchen with a good book when I heard Mr. Jay Jay's feet scrape the window. Within a second, he was standing on the cabinet where Mike had left his pocket change. The jay soon was picking up the shiny nickels, dimes and quarters and dropping them on the counter or the floor. The noise of the coin hitting a hard surface seemed to be a delightful new sound for him. After he had thrown all of the coins on the floor, he flew down and retrieved a dime, which he carried to the dining room window and stuffed into a groove in the frame. Soon this became one of his favorite games, and I often left coins in various places for his entertainment.

"Who's watching me hide my money?"

Very little went unnoticed by the jay, not even a piece of luggage that I was packing for a trip. While I carefully packed the clothes in layers, Mr. Jay Jay disappeared for a few minutes and returned with something in his beak. When I turned around, I noticed that he no longer had the object. He left the room again and reappeared with something else. This time, I decided to watch him, since his frequent trips had raised my curiosity. He hopped on top of the clothes with a coin in his beak and, after looking all about, poked it in among the garments. When I opened my luggage in the hotel, there were coins and tidbits of food in blouse pockets and between skirt pleats. Unpacking always held an element of surprise because I never knew what I might find tucked in my dresses. Although far from home, I couldn't forget my pet.

Mr. Jay Jay always had a fondness for my bedroom. One afternoon he flew in and settled on an antique dresser with a full length mirror and glove boxes. Directly in front of the mirror was a jewelry box, which was just the perfect height for the jay to stand on and see his reflection. In a scene that could have come from a cartoon, he picked a fight with the image. Standing with puffed feathers and erected crest, he lunged at the likeness, striking his beak against the glass. The jay repeated the performance until he became bored and then strutted back and forth as he admired his beauty and proclaimed his victory over the "other bird."

He was intrigued not only by the mirror but by the contents of the jewelry box. When the lid was open, Mr. Jay Jay considered it to be an invitation to enjoy the shiny, sparkling jewelry. He was quite taken with a pair of gold earrings set with a small red stone. When I approached the dresser he left hastily carrying the bauble in his beak. Obviously he had plans to add the sparkling piece to his collection of treasures. Several weeks later I found the earring in the guest bedroom tucked under a pillow.

On some occasions he stole objects that I was not yet ready to part with, which resulted in my hot pursuit. Retrieving the trinket from a bird with tremendous wing power was not an easy job. While I chased the jay, he simply flitted from one curtain rod to another, or to another part of the house, always keeping out of my reach. He knew he was in complete control. This game of his continued until I was breathless and exhausted. He was an accomplished tease and seemed to understand the true meaning of the word.

I sometimes cleaned the house at night. Mr. Jay Jay had an intense dislike for the vacuum cleaner. When it came out of the closet and the motor started up, he flew about squawking and diving at the machine. I wondered whether the noise hurt his ears and disturbed his sleep or, perhaps, he thought the hose was a snake.

I had a tall blue lamp on a table in one of the back bedrooms. Sometimes when I came home, I would find it on the floor. The mystery of how it got there was solved one evening while I cleaned the room. Mr. Jay Jay had learned another trick. By flying with his feet extended forward he was able to knock the lamp to the floor. The combination of his feet and his speed made it possible for him to overturn the lamp by striking it near the top of the shade.

He next tried that trick on a high-back antique chair in the living room. I was away for a few days and when Fran came home that evening the chair was overturned on the floor. This incident greatly concerned her because she thought someone had been in the house in our absence. It was not until later that we actually saw Mr. Jay Jay hit the top of the chair with his feet sending it backwards on the floor. Because the chair was almost balanced, it only took a tap by the jay's feet to overturn it. Until then, I never suspected that my pet was the culprit. Who could have possibly thought a small bird capable of such a prank? I eventually suspected that upsetting the lamp and chair was a way for him to express his displeasure.

On one dreary morning, the beginning of two days of torrential rain, the jay looked outside, ruffled his feathers and decided that additional preening was necessary before venturing out into the wet weather. A day or so before the rain arrived I noticed the jay was conditioning his plumage. Birds appear to have advance warning when inclement weather is moving into the area. Perhaps they have the ability to sense a change in barometric pressure. He carefully preened each feather and treated it with oil he drew from a gland in his body. This served as his "raincoat."

After eating a hearty breakfast, he was ready for another exciting day even though it was a bit wet outside. I opened the door and Mr. Jay Jay headed out to the apple tree. All of a sudden his body moved quickly up and down with his wings quivering while the rain dampened his plumage. Having finished the bath, he shook himself, tipped his head to the side and looked up at the sky as if to say, "The bath was great. Now where is the sunshine?" In a couple of seconds, he flapped off to a row of dense arborvitae trees, apparently seeking more protection from the inclement weather. When the jay arrived for lunch, he showed no further interest in going outdoors.

The kitchen, always a cozy spot for the family to relax, was especially appreciated on this dismal day. A new magazine filled with recipes was the inspiration I needed for making an apple dumpling. While I sat at the table peeling and slicing apples, Mr. Jay Jay carefully inspected them for stray worms. I picked up a wormy apple and placed it in front of him so I could watch his reaction. He cocked his head to the side with a quizzical look and then reduced the apple to tiny bits. It didn't take long for him to find the morsel within. After he swallowed the worm, he glanced up as if to say, "I've finished the main course; where's dessert?"

I had hardly finished sifting the flour into the mixing bowl when I heard a knock on the front door. When I went to the door, I found a gentleman who needed directions to a nearby farm. I was away from the kitchen no more than five minutes, but in that time Mr. Jay Jay had wreaked havoc. I returned to find the cabinet and floor looking as though a tornado had touched down fully loaded with flour. The bird's wings had fanned it in every possible direction. He then flew to the table where he finished shaking the excess flour out of his feathers, sending it all over my antique table.

I found Mr. Jay Jay perched on the door with an impish look in his eye. He always seemed to know when he had been a naughty bird. His crest, instead of standing erect as usual, looked as though it had been glued to his skull. Once I spoke to him, he understood everything was OK and responded by lifting his crest. In spite of the clean-up job, a dreary, rainy afternoon had been brightened by the entertaining antics of my pet. How could such a small bird think of so much mischief?

New behavior patterns emerged as he became more and more devoted to the family. At bedtime he began flying into Fran's room instead of mine. Many items on her dresser attracted his attention, thus giving him a wide choice of toys. He played with trinkets until she was cozily ensconced in bed, then he would fly over and sit on her arm.

When he ruffled his feathers and settled down, we realized that he intended to stay there all night. Being concerned for his safety, I crept into the room after they were both asleep and gently carried Mr. Jay Jay to his perch. From that time on, he preferred to sleep with, not just near, his adopted family.

On several occasions I was awakened by shrieks during the night. The first time this happened, I quickly switched on the bedside lamp, and prepared to treat a sick bird. But Mr. Jay Jay was not ill. He was not even awake! I went back to sleep without solving the mystery. Three or four weeks later, the same thing occurred, only there was a louder shriek. Because it was a moonlit night, I could see around the room without turning on a lamp. While I watched, his wings twitched, his body jerked and he made jay noises, yet he was still asleep. I decided that Mr. Jay Jay was having a nightmare. When I spoke to him, he recognized my voice. He then quickly jerked his wings, making a flicking sound, similar to that of a rattlesnake, fluffed his feathers and settled down for a more restful sleep. I never figured out the reason he flicked his wings unless it was some type of warning or he was ready for instant flight.

One thing that separated him from most humans is that he never watched much television. He did notice when we got a new set, however. He arrived in the room and seemed to have a questioning expression as he watched from the curtain. In a few minutes, he was strutting to and fro on top of the set, pausing occasionally to peck the control buttons. All at once, he skidded to a halt, stretched his neck out and leaned over the side to look at the picture. The old set was black and white and the new one was color. The jay knew something was different. After he had satisfied his curiosity he flew over to me, and life returned to normal.

The experience raised a question in my mind: Is it possible for birds to recognize pictorial images? I have also had peafowl that would venture up onto the patio and stand there for a long time looking through the glass door at television. Maybe they prefer wildlife programs!

Chapter Four

Autumn Surprises

The Virginia countryside was bathed in the soft amber colors of early autumn. Maple, oak and gum trees were clad in hues of orange, red and yellow foliage. Sumac bushes were blazing with orange-red foliage, outlining the fields against the woodlands. The air was cool and crisp. Fields of goldenrod, fall daisies and patches of purple asters glowed as if touched by an artist's brush.

The first V-shaped flock of Canada geese honked overhead, echoing across the countryside and forecasting the weather changes to come. These geese seem to fly over every year at about the time of the Autumnal Equinox. That first flock announces the coming of fall. The changing season also reminded me that Mr. Jay Jay could become a part of this movement. Each day I saw feathered creatures as they passed by, heading south. Migration is an incredible exhibition of endurance.

Even though the air is hazy and humid with the remains of summer, the migration of birds stirs it with the mysteries of nature. The numerous birds involved in this seasonal movement are amazing and the distances they cover are beyond belief. Migration appears as a continuing journey of birds to southern latitudes. Approximately seventy five percent of mating birds in our area migrate to some degree. They leave to escape the cold winters and to seek a plentiful supply of food. These trips involve dangerous conditions, and not all of them make it. Each year I see many newcomers at my feeder as they migrate. In spite of the perilous trip, migration is necessary for the success of many species.

The ruby-throated hummingbird is just one example. This tiny bird makes an extended flight across the Gulf of Mexico to winter in Central America, returning to its summer home about the time azaleas begin blooming in our area. It travels across this unmarked expanse as we could not without a map or compass.

Toward the end of summer I noticed hummers tanking up on food at the sugar-water feeder that hangs near my kitchen window. They seem to have an insatiable appetite, draining the bottle every few days. I have heard, as a gentle reminder that the feeder is empty, whirring wings just above my head. There may be several reasons for their hunger: a scarcity of flowers producing nectar and the need to stock up for their long journey.

Nature endowed migratory birds with some special sense that enables them to cross vast areas without becoming lost. Some think these birds use the sun and stars and natural objects to stay on course. Whatever the explanation, birds appear to be born with an internal compass. They know where they want to fly and how to get there.

The first blush of dawn promised another bright, cool day. The sun peeked above the horizon, imparting a rosy glow to the sky. The birds were awakening the world with their morning songs.

Mr. Jay Jay began his morning by stretching one wing and one leg at a time. This signaled his readiness for the events of the day, starting with breakfast. As soon as we finished eating, the jay was off to play and I was off to work. That particular morning I drove the station wagon to work instead of the van. My florist shop was in the back corner of a shopping center, eight miles from my home.

When I got to the store at 9 a.m., it was such a beautiful autumn day that I left the front door open to let in fresh air and sunlight. After preparing the store for business, I began to make fresh floral arrangements and to plan the route for morning deliveries. In addition to those jobs, there were customers who needed help, both in the store and on the telephone.

At about 9:30, I heard Mike's dump truck as he drove into the shopping center and parked just beyond my car. He had finished picking up greenhouse supplies in town and stopped by for a quick cup of coffee before going back home. Shortly after Mike left the store, a customer entered. The customer completed her purchase and was leaving, when the telephone rang and I answered it. In the next instant, a jay bird sailed over the customer's head and alighted on the plant booth just inside the door. The lady ducked her head and muttered something under her breath in complete astonishment.

I wondered whether I was actually seeing Mr. Jay Jay or if it were a different blue jay. As soon as I spoke to him, he fluttered off the plant booth and landed on my shoulder. It was difficult to believe that he had flown eight miles, and was now sitting on my shoulder at ten o'clock in the morning.

After considerable thought, I concluded that he must have followed either my vehicle or Mike's dump truck. The old truck was a trifle noisy and, after all, the jay had helped repair it. I believe the jay heard my voice while I talked to the customer in the store and on the telephone, thereby guiding him to the right shop.

When I regained my composure, I carried my pet into the bathroom for his own safety. Thinking no one would believe my story; I phoned the photographer I had worked with on weddings, and briefly described what had just happened. Mr. Jay Jay's escapade had been an autumn surprise that needed documentation.

Being only a short distance away, the photographer soon arrived at the store with camera in hand and a bemused expression on his face. The bathroom was not exactly the ideal studio, but he managed to take several photographs of the jay perched on my shoulder.

Being confined in such a small area was not Mr. Jay Jay's idea of fun. Each time I visited, he appeared to be sulking and would only utter an occasional disgruntled "Jaeeh." In an effort to make him happier, I devised a makeshift perch in front of the mirror and attached some shiny odds and ends. The toys and the shared contents of my lunchbox lifted his spirit and adjusted his attitude.

In mid-afternoon as I watered the flower planters outside the door, I noticed some grasshoppers on the plants. I caught several and offered them to my pet. The choice tidbits quelled his appetite until he was home again.

At closing time, I placed Mr. Jay Jay in a box for

the eight-mile trip back to the farm. Traveling in a box must have been a humiliating experience that bruised his pride. While we rode along, I could hear the thump, thump of his feet on the cardboard. I tried to console him by talking and whistling a tune. Even though the jay was in a carton, he knew the minute the car turned into the lane.

As soon as we were inside the house, I opened the box and he sprang upward, like a jack-in-the-box. He flew from room to room making jubilant shrieks. That was the first and last trip Mr. Jay Jay made to town.

His experience convinced me that birds do have the ability to know where they are in this extensive world. It also taught me that they can judge direction. These abilities allow them to make cognitive decisions regarding their destination and how to achieve their goals.

On the afternoon of September 29, Mike telephoned the store and asked me to come home. When I arrived, he told me that my father had passed away. I would have to leave for southern Virginia and my family home.

Mr. Jay Jay had apparently heard my car as it came up the driveway. Within seconds, he was in the front yard. While I walked toward the house, he flew around to the kitchen window. By the time I reached the bedroom he was landing on my dresser. My pet followed me from place to place as I hastily packed my clothes. He seemed once again to perceive my intentions, and my sadness.

I knew we would be away for three days and the jay had never been alone for that long. I made provisions for him by leaving the window open and giving him access to his food and water. I bid my pet goodbye and left him in the house.

A few days later, driving back from southern Virginia, my thoughts turned to Mr. Jay Jay. By the time I got home, it was late afternoon. When I stepped from the car, I heard the jay in the direction of the rock garden. I had barely opened the front door, when he headed straight for my shoulder. He cocked his head up and uttered a soft "Jaeeh" greeting that immediately lifted my spirits.

September and October bring many changes. It is a time when man and other creatures prepare for winter, saying goodbye to one season while anticipating another. Birds that remain for a part of the winter, or for all of it, also prepare for the bitter months ahead. Their instincts help them to select sheltered roosting spots and likely food sources.

With the seasonal change, also came the task of preparing the gardens for winter rest. The cooler weather gave me the boost I needed to begin that project. The first area I chose to work on was around the birdbath, for it was here that I had planted annual flowers, which now had the look of death upon them and needed to be removed.

While I pulled and clipped dead stems, Mr. Jay Jay perched on a wild cherry branch overhanging the birdbath. When I looked up he was intently eyeing the shimmering water. He approached cautiously while looking for intruders.

After a brief glance around the garden, the jay decided that a bath was a good idea. He sailed to the rim of the birdbath and took the plunge, landing chest deep in the water. He first took a cool drink, then dipped his beak and shook his head from side to side, throwing water onto his back. While he splashed the water with his tail, his fluttering wings set up a string of ripples that rolled over the edge of the birdbath. After bobbing up and down repeatedly, he stepped up on the rim, leaving the birdbath almost empty.

With his outer feathers soaked, he struggled to reach a branch in the cherry tree. He shook off the excess water and began oiling his plumage. By twisting his tail to one side, he was able to reach his oil gland and collect the oil in his beak. The jay then rubbed the oil into all of his feathers. I watched as he wiped the oil on his foot and then scratched his head, thus oiling this difficult spot. After he finished picking and smoothing his feathers, he flew to a cedar tree.

A bird's feathers serve many essential needs. They protect the bird against cold inclement weather, regulate proper body heat, and enable the bird to fly. Well-maintained plumage plays a role in courtship behavior as well as improving their chance for survival.

Birds need water in the winter just as they do

in the summer. A shallow concrete birdbath with gently sloping sides can be left out all year. Freezing water will not damage this type of bath; mine has been in continuous use for twenty years.

My family has never seemed to regret the departure of summer, because the comfortable autumn days are a welcome relief from the stifling heat and humidity here in Virginia. When the leaves and acorns begin tumbling down, we generally spend an afternoon picking up pieces of broken limbs and twigs in preparation for raking the leaves. We reconcile ourselves to the fact that what falls down must be picked up.

We were actively engaged in raking leaves into piles while Mr. Jay Jay was occupied with picking up white oak acorns and flying away with them to one of his secret spots. Until then, I had not noticed his keen interest in an outside larder. He was stashing provisions in anticipation of winter. In between finding acorns and hiding them, he sat on a limb, squawked to his friends and then drifted down to hitch a ride on my shoulder.

On the morning of October 10, the temperature

dropped suddenly from pleasantly cool to cold—a drastic change from the previous day. A pewter gray sky and stillness in the air indicated that snow was not far away. By 8 AM, wet snow had begun falling, covering the ground and placing a heavy burden on trees that still clung to their leaves. I could not remember when snow had fallen so early in the fall.

While Mr. Jay Jay waited for a hearty breakfast, he sat at the window looking out at the snow-covered ground. When we finished eating, I opened the door, but he showed no interest in venturing outside. It was an autumn surprise, one the jay had not experienced before.

Just a few days earlier, I had moved the bird feeder from the side yard to the pear tree at the back of the house, where it could be seen more easily from the kitchen table. As the snow tapered off, leaving a three-inch accumulation, the birds began to arrive at their restaurant. Mr. Jay Jay was content to sit inside and watch. If one of his friends swooped too close, he pulled his feathers tightly against his body and ducked his head. After what he perceived to be several close encounters, he began "Jaeehing" harshly, as if answering his buddies. At last he couldn't stand the excitement any longer and flew over to the door. I knew then that he was eager for a new adventure.

I watched intently for the jay's feet to touch the snow. He was a comical sight as his feet settled into the fluffy white stuff, sinking him chest-deep. With a flutter of wings, he lifted straight up in the air and flew to a nearby tree. After regaining his composure, he shook himself and headed to the feeder. The moment he landed, there was fierce competition from a couple of mockingbirds that were enjoying a suet cake on the feeder and an apple I had placed in the tree. In spite of being outnumbered, the jay put forth a courageous fight, giving me the impression that he had engaged in earlier skirmishes. Other than losing a few small feathers, he was unscathed. My pet then claimed his uncontested spot on the feeder, rapidly picking up numerous sunflower seeds before flying away. Jays do tend to be somewhat aggressive toward other birds when feeding and Mr. Jay Jay's behavior at the feeder was true to form. When he became tired of scrapping with the ruffians, he was ready to come back inside.

Chapter Five

Instinctive Awakening

It was the first cold, windy day in November and Mr. Jay Jay was in no rush to go outdoors. I noticed that the area outside the back door was at last free of summer clutter and that the lawn was almost clean. The few remaining leaves would soon be swept into the woods or under the shrubs by a brisk wind. The trees had been stripped of their foliage and through them I had an early preview of what was yet to come. After Mike mowed the fields the little valley beyond the house could be seen.

In spite of the chill, we left the window open, giving Mr. Jay Jay complete freedom to come and go at will. He had been a part of our family for five months, and his daily habits were well established. Observing his development and behavior was an educational experience. Mr. Jay Jay continued to enjoy the best of both worlds.

Nature had been preparing the jay for the upcoming winter, replacing his tattered feathers with bright new ones. Jay birds usually begin molting in August. As old feathers were gradually lost new ones replaced the old plumage, never leaving Mr. Jay Jay with bald spots on his body. Feathers that are just emerging from the bird's skin are known as pinfeathers. The short fluffy down next to his body was, for him the equivalent of thermal underwear. His colored feathers were no longer the dull blue of an immature bird; instead, he sported bright blue ones. The mature plumage would also help him advertise for a mate.

Mr. Jay Jay's voice was no longer limited to a raucous squawk and other imitations. With maturity came softer songs, one of which resembled that of a meadowlark. Jays tend to be fairly quiet in the summer, but become more vocal as autumn draws near. Songs are extremely important in attracting a mate and in their courtship. Even though Mr. Jay Jay learned different songs and new calls, I was always able to distinguish his voice from other jays by the rapidity of his "Jaeehs."

Instinct—an inborn behavior pattern—urged the jay to forage for food in the outside environment, even though he was well supplied in the house. When he had hidden acorns while we raked the yard, this innate sense had been at work. He had recognized them as food and had cached the nuts outside for winter use. I realized the significance of his action; it was an instinct awakening.

As autumn progressed and daylight grew shorter, the jay was home most afternoons before I returned from work. However, on one occasion I arrived home and he was not in his usual spot. I found him in the kitchen with his crest straight up, looking as if he had been naughty. By mistake I had left a small bag of unshelled peanuts on the cabinet that morning. Much to my surprise, he had not only found the nuts, but had pecked a hole in the plastic bag and proceeded to eat and hide half the contents. I was more amused than angry because he reminded me of a mischievous child who got caught with his hand in the cookie jar.

Along with fall came our craving for pumpkin pie and Mike brought in a pumpkin and placed it on the kitchen table. The jay had never seen a pumpkin before. When the knife sliced through the meat, exposing the inside, Mr. Jay Jay hurried over for a closer look. Mike scraped the fat seeds from the inner wall and put them on a piece of newspaper, while Mr. Jay Jay watched from his shoulder. The bird knew at once that it was edible, and snatched a seedy portion, leaving a messy trail as he flew away. His instinctive ability to detect food was becoming highly developed.

In November, I became aware that the jay's interest in outside activities had intensified. Each morning he gobbled down his breakfast and without delay flew to the door, demanding his daily freedom. That pattern continued for several weeks before I understood the reason for his haste.

One morning during breakfast, I noticed another blue jay in the apple tree near the window. The bird gave a couple of "Jaeeh" shrieks, which prompted Mr.

Jay Jay to fly about the room with no further interest in his food. I opened the door and he sailed outside to the same tree, perching only a few feet away from the other bird. The new bird in town stared at my pet, seemingly entranced, its head turning as it watched every move he made. A few minutes later Mr. Jay Jay gave a loud call and they soared over the field toward the woods. After thinking about his behavior, I concluded the stranger was a female.

After observing their routine for a week, I was convinced that Mr. Jay Jay was engaged in a serious courtship. She arrived each morning at about the same time. Her call never failed to fill him with ardent zeal, which sent me scurrying over to open the door for him. Sometimes he flew nonchalantly from one limb to the other and sometimes he would flit back and forth faster and faster, as if trying to get her attention. He made an occasional boisterous squawk when he changed course. Her little black eyes never lost sight of him. I was now certain that they were a pair.

He was only five months old when the mating instinct began to awaken. I was unaware that this desire would mature at such an early age. I had anticipated that the selection of a mate would begin in March. Because of Mr. Jay Jay's emerging behavior, I could only wonder how long he would continue to live in a dual world. Only the jay knew the time when he would respond to the sign of the season and the call of the wild. In the meantime, I enjoyed and appreciated each incredible day I spent with him.

Although he was sharing his life with a girl friend now, he arrived home most evenings before the trees were outlined against the fading sky. He continued to learn new things and to entertain us with his tricks. He still wanted to be with his adopted family in the evenings and there was no noticeable change in his personality.

The ringing of a telephone always got the jay's attention. He was smart enough to know that the sound demanded a response on our part. If it was not answered by the third or fourth ring, he flew to the phone and frantically pecked the old-fashioned rotary dial. As soon as I lifted the receiver, he hopped to my shoulder to share the conversation.

"Excuse me, I'd like to make a call."

He eventually learned to rotate the dial with his beak.

On chilly nights in November we enjoyed the fireplace in the living room. The hearthside opening was covered by a fire-screen, making it safe for use around the jay. He watched from the curtain rod while I crumpled paper and placed kindling and wood on the andirons. When I put a match to it and the material burst into flames, he appeared to be upset by the sudden roar of the fire. After it died down, I sat on the hearth with Mr. Jay Jay on my shoulder to lessen his concern. Because of his smug, contented look, it was obvious he had recovered from his momentary fright and he, too, enjoyed the warmth. The jay soon discovered that the fireplace set was the perfect place to sit and warm his hind parts. He seemed to appreciate the coziness and shared the excitement by flying about the room whenever I began to lay a fire.

During the latter part of November, I came home one evening to find that the jay was not in the house. I had expected that to happen after the girl friend put in her appearance, so it came as no surprise. But there was always the possibility of a mishap, and that concerned me. It was also the first time that Mr. Jay Jay had stayed outdoors on a cold night. When I retired for the evening, I could only hope that the jay was tucked away in a dense evergreen to protect his body from the cold, blustery wind.

The following evening, his happy voice greeted me from his usual look-out post, the dining room window. He appeared glad to be inside the house preceding me to the kitchen. While I prepared our food, he played with his toys and occasionally mimicked an unfamiliar bird call. Several days later, I was able to identify the new call.

From the north window, I looked out onto the back yard and saw a sparrow hawk perched in the pear tree above the bird feeder. This bird, also known as a kestrel, preys on mice, insects and songbirds. In a short time I heard a series of raucous jay shrieks and realized that Mr. Jay Jay was actually alerting all of the birds in the yard area to the impending danger. Maybe my pet had encountered a small problem with that predator and that was the reason for some of his overnight excursions.

In the days that followed, the jay's playful outdoor conduct appeared to cause some annoyance among the songbirds. He appeared to take great delight in giving an occasional sparrow hawk or red tailed-hawk imitation, which he followed with a string of rapid "Jaeeh" calls. He gave me the impression he was playing the double role of "good-guy, bad-guy."

His mischievous use of a predatory call sent the songbirds scattering in every direction for cover. Perhaps it was a clever method of ridding the birdfeeder of his competition. The hawk incident could have been an instinctive reaction. His instinct alerted him to the danger of predatory birds, but his keen intelligence allowed him to use the knowledge to his own advantage. It was another lesson Mr. Jay Jay had learned about survival in the outside world.

With the Thanksgiving holiday only a day away, there was an additional flurry of activity in the household that morning. The jay was in a skittish mood and flashed about the kitchen, bouncing off everything in sight. He seemed to perceive that I was occupied with projects that were a bit different from my customary chores. His girl friend called for him at the regular time, but Mr. Jay Jay didn't show his usual enthusiasm. When I opened the door, he reluctantly left the house and headed toward the pond with his friend following only a few feet behind him.

Most of the afternoon was gone when I began to set the table for the festive occasion. Very shortly I heard bird feet touch down on the sill and a soft "Jaeeh" as he ducked in through the window. My pet watched intently while I placed the silver, china and crystal on the table. The addition of the tiny silver salt spoons completed the setting and I returned to the kitchen, forgetting the devilish jay who sat quietly watching every move. Nothing escaped his sharp eyes.

Twenty or thirty minutes later I realized I had not seen nor heard Mr. Jay Jay. He had evidently perched on top of the corner cupboard instead of the drapery and my eyes missed him when I left the room. I was reminded of my mother's old familiar saying: "An idle mind is the Devil's workshop." With this thought, I peeked around the corner and found him sitting on the table with a salt spoon in his beak.

While I had forgotten about him, my little devil had been at work. When I took count of the small spoons, one was already missing besides the one he had in his beak. Not wanting to spend the remainder of the afternoon searching for two tiny spoons, I approached him slowly, with kind, gentle words. The jay cocked his head and looked at me as if to say, "This must be some sort of game." Up went his crest and, with a "Catch me if you can" attitude, he sailed off to another room carrying the new found treasure.

Upon inspection of the table, I found the missing spoon hidden under a napkin. The rumpled napkin was a dead giveaway. Jays and crows are attracted to shiny objects. This reminded me of an incident my grandmother had with a crow she nursed back to health. He went visiting and returned home with a silver spoon.

There are always last-minute preparations for the traditional holiday dinner. This year was no exception, so Mr. Jay Jay and I awoke at dawn on Thanksgiving Day. As soon as he finished breakfast, I invited him out of the house. For that reason he was out and about long before his companion arrived. His eyes scanned the sky while he waited for her in the pear tree. After playing a waiting game and neither seeing nor hearing her, he made a couple of irritated shrieks and took off to the woods.

A short time after he left the yard, I heard her "Jaeehing." Receiving no answer, she flew over to the window to look for him. Her concern was obvious as she squawked, flitted and hopped about nervously in the apple tree. With a sudden flutter of wings, she lifted off and headed in the direction of the tall trees at the edge of the woods. She had heard the song she was listening for.

My family began to arrive for dinner in the early afternoon. When I walked outside to greet them, I heard the jay announcing his presence from overhead. The gravel driveway had sounded their arrival and his acute ears had recognized the sound of a strange vehicle. He had returned to the yard to investigate.

Once the guests were inside, Mr. Jay Jay hustled around to the back of the house and slipped through the open window. He was so full of curiosity that he never paused in the kitchen. Instead, he quickly flew to the living room and shrieked his noisy greeting to everyone present. They had just received their first introduction and, I must say, there were a few raised eyebrows.

Not knowing how my pet would react to a house filled with company, I had hoped he would stay outside with his friend until we finished dinner. Of course, that was too much to expect. The ever-perceptive jay was not easily fooled.

After catching up on some of the family news, my brother Ted and I went to the kitchen and began the remaining preparations for the meal. We were unaware that Mr. Jay Jay had followed us. He perched on the door and with great interest watched each knife stroke as Ted carved the Thanksgiving turkey.

Just as Ted cut the last slice and put the knife on the platter, the jay decided that the visitor was no longer welcome. He flew down and raked his feet through Ted's carefully combed hair. I had to laugh; the little imp had waited until my brother had finished carving before he invited the stranger out of "his kitchen." Ted's expression was a classic example of complete surprise.

I served the jay's Thanksgiving meal, placed it on the kitchen table, and closed the door to the dining room. I thought this would avoid any further behavior problems during dinner. He ate his food and quietly, sneaked out the window for the rest of the afternoon with his friend.

Each day, the instinctive awakenings within Mr. Jay Jay were more and more evident. The call of love was fascinating to observe as it progressed from one stage to another. The jay and his companion were together from morning to dusk, soaring over fields and woods, sharing their beauty and joy with the rest of the world. It was apparent to me that a marriage was imminent.

Chapter Six

Christmas With Mr. Jay Jay

December was the time for Christmas magic in the kitchen and through our home. Mr. Jay Jay's life was filled with new surprises each day as I prepared for the holidays. During that time, the kitchen was his chosen spot, for there aromas filled the air and sharpened his appetite.

Most of the holiday baking was done in the evenings or on Sunday. Even though he was eager to go outside each morning, he made frequent trips back to check on the progress in the kitchen. That particular day I planned to make a fruitcake and let the jay out early. He and Miss Jay played in the yard and then flew to the woods. In a short time, they were back in the pear tree and within minutes he was on the window, peering into the kitchen. When he realized I was cooking, he sneaked inside, leaving her in the tree. He hopped over to the window and bobbed up and down as if trying to coax her to come in. He was unpersuasive and she soon flew away.

Once his eyes lit on the fruitcake ingredients, he was no longer interested in being outdoors. While I measured the nuts, raisins and assorted fruits, Mr. Jay Jay looked on with eager eyes. It was only a matter of time before he sampled the ingredients. This time his first choice was a raisin instead of a nut. He next snatched a piece of candy from the dish by the TV and flew to the curtain rod. The candy didn't sit too well and he dropped it. Birds have the ability not only to taste food, but to smell it. It was interesting to note that he never ate citrus fruit; in fact, if we offered him a bit of citrus he would shake his head and fly away.

After sampling a few of the raisins, he picked up several and vanished in the direction of his storage room. But when he came back for more, they had disappeared into the cake batter. He hopped

Fruit cake samplings

onto the cabinet, stretched his neck and carefully inspected each empty bowl, as if asking, "Where are the goodies?" The jay looked so disappointed that I just had to spoil him with a few more from the box.

From Mr. Jay Jay, I learned that many birds have a great fondness for a variety of fruits in either their fresh or dried form. Apples, raisins, apricots and pears were consistent favorites. I frequently placed these on the feeder, especially during the cold winter months when wild fruits are not readily available. The natural sugar contained in this type of food is a valuable source of energy. I have seen birds in our area eating holly, juniper, poke and honeysuckle berries when the ground is covered with snow. These wild creatures appreciate our treats.

As the Yule season drew near, I made my annual pilgrimage to the attic in search of the Christmas paraphernalia stored there. To do this, I had to pull down the disappearing stairs. When I began that project, Mr. Jay Jay was relaxing in the kitchen. While I sat on the attic floor, sorting through piles of gift boxes and shiny decorations, I suddenly heard a flutter of wings and a squawk. Looking down, I saw my pet flying straight up the steps into the attic. The space was poorly lit and he fluttered slowly over to a clothes rod, as if feeling his way through the murky light.

After watching for a few minutes, he glided down and landed right in the midst of what he must surely have considered a sparkling treasure trove. He began to pull out bits of paper and ribbons, finally choosing a silver ribbon with an attached small bell. Mr. Jay Jay played happily with this trinket, tapping it up and down on the floor. The tinkling sound of the bell seemed to fascinate him.

While he was playing, he managed to get the ribbon wrapped around his foot. This alarmed him, and he decided that flying was the best way to free himself. As he flew about the attic, the tinkling sound of the bell followed him. When he determined that flight was not the answer, he settled down on the clothes rod. While he looked at the dangling bell with a wary eye, the jay picked up his foot and tried to untwist the ribbon.

I realized that my pet was in quite a predicament.

I held out my hand and called him but he refused to fly anywhere. So I carefully made my way through all the boxes and wrappings to reach him. He sat calmly as I untangled his foot, never once moving a feather or attempting to peck me, even though he was most certainly upset.

The jay had inside adventures and his days outside were filled with romance. On a frosty morning in mid-December, while I looked out at the rock garden, I saw Mr. Jay Jay and Miss Jay fly to the redbud tree in the garden. After quickly glancing about the area as if checking for predators, they settled down to the ground and scuttled under some low juniper branches. The jays began to rake their beaks through the shrubs, tossing them in all directions as they looked beneath each leaf.

It was evident to me that Mr. Jay Jay had previously stored food there and had now returned to retrieve it. In a short time, he located what was perhaps an acorn or peanut, and holding the tidbit in his beak, tenderly offered it to his sweetheart. She made little "Jaeeh" noises, accepted his token of love, and flitted off to a tree to enjoy the morsel.

After seeing them sharing their food, I knew the romance was growing more intense.

Decorating for the holidays was a time of high spirits and happiness. While I brought containers of fresh greenery and boxes of ornaments into the living room, the jay gingerly watched the activity. His colossal curiosity, with an eye that noticed every change, created some interesting moments.

The living room was the first area to be transformed for the festive occasion. A hand-painted Nativity set always graced the long mantel, reflecting the joyous mood of the season. The set was centered in front of a large mirror with an angel suspended above the crèche. Pine, magnolia, and holly greenery, in addition to cones and candles, embellished the ends of the mantel. With arrangements on the coffee table and piano, the living-room decorations were almost complete. The only thing missing was the Christmas tree.

Leaving the jay in the living room, I gathered up the remaining greenery and hurried outside to trim the patio. A green garland with red berries was draped along the railing and a swag for the door

"The crèche got my curiosity up."

added the finishing touches to the exterior. With only a minor adjustment to the swag, I hastened inside to enjoy the comfort of a cheerful fire.

I glanced at the curtain and did not see the jay. I slowly scanned the room and caught sight of him. He had found the Nativity set and was perched on top of the crèche, staring with rapt interest at the angel suspended above his head. I imagined the figurines lying on the hearth, smashed to a million pieces, but he did not overturn a single one. Mr. Jay Jay's presence actually added a quality of animation to the figures in the manger scene. Unfortunately, the camera was not in my hand.

The selection of a Christmas tree was one of our favorite pursuits. We usually made it a family outing and would spend several hours looking at and debating the appearance of a variety of different candidates. Since we were not growing Christmas trees we had to ramble about the farm looking for the perfect native pine. Mr. Jay Jay soon joined us. While we walked along, he flew side-by-side with us or hitched a ride on a convenient shoulder. Whenever we paused to consider a particular tree, he took advantage of the opportunity by resting on the top branches and "Jaeehing" his opinion.

After what felt like miles of walking, we finally found a pine that met all our criteria. As the pruning saw bit into the bark, the tree began to sway underneath Mr. Jay Jay's feet. Up went his crest and, just as he darted away, the tree crashed to the ground with a swooshing sound. Having an apparently solid, stable tree fall from under his feet must have been a disconcerting moment for the jay.

When trees are standing in the field, they always appear smaller than they actually are. Our choice that year was no exception. Once we got the tree to the patio, we realized the size was a bit of a problem. While Mike tugged and pulled, trying to get it into the living room, Mr. Jay Jay attempted to fly around the annoying obstacle. After several attempts, he gave up and opted for a free ride in on its branches. As Mike dragged the tree through the doorway, I had to smile at the jay that adorned its boughs.

Once inside, the jay flew to the curtain rod above the sofa for a better view of all the activity. The tree was placed in a stand and then secured to the wall to prevent Mr. Jay Jay from knocking it over. The previous year, the fully decorated tree had fallen over when there was no bird in the house. With the jay's curiosity, I knew that it was just a matter of time before he checked it out.

Sure enough, we had barely cleared the room when I heard the Jay take to the air. I peeped around the corner and saw him circling the tree with an expression of pure pleasure. He seemed to be saying, "I finally got a real perch in this place." After making a final inspection, he settled on one of the branches, obviously quite at home. This was certainly the best of two worlds.

Of course, without ornaments, even the most beautiful spruce pine is just another tree. Our collection had begun with odds and ends of lights, glass balls and other treasured childhood decorations. I did wonder how the Christmas trimmings could weather the storm that was now perched in the tree. We waited until the jay had retired for the night to complete the tree trimming.

The next morning Mr. Jay Jay was up bright and early; I, too, crawled out early in order to protect our ornaments. His first stop was the kitchen, in search of food. Having satisfied that need, the next place on his itinerary was the living room. I sneaked into an adjoining room, which had a mirror that was ideally located for spying on my pet. I tried to be quiet, but after a few minutes, I could no longer control my laughter. When he discovered a fully decorated tree, he flitted by, circled back and gently tapped a glass ball with his feet. His wing power and speed created air currents when he flew near the tree, and that made the tinsel shimmer and set the ornaments swinging to and fro. He was smart enough to recognize that his flight resulted in the movement of the various trimmings, and he used this information to the best of his ability. The jay visited the living room frequently but never broke a single item. Because of his enjoyment, I didn't interfere with his Christmas spirit.

Although Mr. Jay Jay had been kept busy with Christmas decorating, he hadn't forsaken his sweetheart. The jay's companion usually arrived at the well-stocked bird feeder for breakfast, before calling him to the window. She could easily see him from the feeder and exchange morning greetings. When she had finished eating, she hurried to the pear tree and called excitedly, announcing that she was ready to play. This was what he had been listening for, and he shot outside.

Late afternoon the sky was streaked with shades of orange and pink as the sun dropped behind the holly trees. Mr. Jay Jay got home as the last ray of light faded into dusk. He was a little late and, as always, this caused a few anxious moments, reminding me that someday he might fly away and never return.

On a chilly evening just before the Yuletide, the children and I decided to take a respite from the hustle and bustle of the season. While we sat by a crackling fire, sipping eggnog and sampling cookies, the jay entertained us with his playful mischief. The telephone briefly interrupted our relaxation. When we returned my pet was perched on the rim of my cup, taking a few sips of eggnog. He knew that he had been a roguish bird and left immediately. Not certain how much he had consumed, I was somewhat concerned about the consequences. I

A sip of coffee this morning

watched him closely to make sure he didn't suffer any ill effects from imbibing the holiday cheer. The only thing I noticed was a nodding head as he drifted off to sleep.

The next morning Mr. Jay Jay was in fine spirits, having suffered no lingering effects from his imprudence the previous evening. The jay evidently liked the eggnog. I usually drank a cup of coffee while I prepared breakfast. When I looked toward the table the jay's head was in my cup sampling the last sip. After he enjoyed breakfast and coffee, he was ready for another day with his sweetie. He went into gyrations when he heard her sweet voice; that sent me hustling to open the door.

Candlelight in the dining room was a traditional part of our Christmas décor. There were candles on both the table and the sideboard. When I placed the candles, I had a feeling of doubt. After all, the jay did share the house.

The first holiday dinner was planned for December 23. Mr. Jay Jay came home late in the afternoon to offer a helping beak in the kitchen. As soon as he heard cars and strange voices, he

And a napkin for my beak

hastened to the living room. I knew he was up to his usual mischief. The jay was showing off his newly discovered prank by flying at the tree and tapping the ornaments with his feet. That brought forth appreciative laughter from his audience, which he appeared to enjoy thoroughly.

The candles burned brightly, adding a festive touch to the dining area. I made a last minute inspection of the table and announced dinner. As our guests entered the room, Mr. Jay Jay zipped over their heads to claim his spot on the cornice. I accepted this impish caper and hoped that he would stay out of trouble.

I had hardly picked up my fork when my pet's body language told me that he was ready to pull another trick out of his bag. All at once, he swooped down with great speed and flitted past a candle on the table, extinguishing the flame. Before I could chase him out, he made a second pass over a candle on the sideboard, extinguishing that one also. That was enough and the jay was sent to the kitchen for the balance of the evening.

The next evening, I lit the candles again and

Mr. Jay Jay methodically put them out, one by one. I concluded that he had either clipped the flame with the tip of his wing or the down draft of air he created snuffed it. I wondered if he perceived the candle flames to be a danger.

On Christmas Eve morning we were greeted with a magnificent sunrise. The eastern sky filled with a warm glow of rose and salmon colors, helping to balance the frigid temperature. In spite of the cold, the jay was eagerly waiting to join his friend. He seemed well adapted to the extreme weather.

By mid-afternoon, the fitful wind switched and began to blow from the north, sending the thermometer into a nose dive. As I poured the last layer of topping on the salad, I heard several taps at the window. Looking up, I saw the jay standing on the sill asking to come inside. I opened the window and he scurried into the kitchen; he, too, was home for the holidays.

Shortly after the jay returned, our family began to arrive. As soon as he heard the first knock on the door, he was off to the living room "Jaeehing" his greeting. This time Mr. Jay Jay demonstrated how fast he could fly past the tree while dodging the ornaments. He had learned "defensive flying techniques" at a tender age by flitting in between the legs and rungs of the kitchen chairs.

Mr. Jay Jay's shrieks roused the household early Christmas morning. Before long, all activity was centered in the living room. Both young and older folks were filled with anticipation as they waited to open the gifts beneath the tree. The jay looked with a dubious eye as I placed his stocking on the coffee table. With a bit of coaxing he glided down and peered inside the stocking, which contained shiny trinkets, nuts and of course raisins. After stuffing himself on Christmas treats, he was kept busy hiding the new earrings and buttons.

Preparation for the feast began early in the morning and by mid-afternoon all were waiting to enjoy the meal. Just as we began to serve dinner, my pet jay scrambled through the window and, within seconds, was sitting on the back of my chair. He waited there for a few minutes. Then, he hopped onto the table, snatched a piece of food and scuttled right through the middle of my plate. I was more than surprised by his table manners and glad that only family members were present. Mr. Jay Jay was again the center of attention as a burst of laughter filled the room.

When the celebration ended and the last car had rolled down the driveway, I sank into a comfortable chair to reflect on the memorable occasion. The combination of a warm, glowing fire and a tired body soon put me to sleep. An hour or so later, I awoke to find my beloved jay resting on my shoulder. He too had been snoozing by the fire. Our Christmas was over and once again quiet settled over the household.

Chapter Seven

His Final Choice

Christmas was only a pleasant memory as January ushered in a season of tranquility. As the days lengthened, each afternoon a little longer than the last, I indulged in one of my favorite pastimes. I relaxed by the fire, surrounded by spring gardening catalogs as I planned my new garden that would fill my spring, summer and fall days with all the colors in nature's palette.

The first week of the New Year brought us unseasonably balmy temperatures and Miss Jay began displaying a touch of spring fever. It tended to be Mr. Jay Jay's custom to carry on his courtship throughout the day and very properly return home at night. It seemed that the jay's chosen mate was becoming impatient with his split lifestyle—in the house at night and your typical free-flying jaybird during the day. Each morning she arrived at the back door, seemingly earlier than the day before, insisting in ear-splitting squawks that he leave his human home and pay her some attention.

The jays were frequent flyers between the yard and other unknown places, endlessly traveling back and forth. On several passes through the back yard, Mr. Jay Jay swept near me as if to settle on my shoulder but swerved and flew elsewhere with his new mate. I knew he wasn't timid, so either he was just teasing me or he was intimidated by his companion. I suppose no self-respecting courting jay would want to be called a momma's bird.

Out of Miss Jay's sight, he was his regular affectionate self. He continued to greet me, from his normal location, where he could watch the driveway. While we were in the kitchen preparing and eating dinner he was busy checking out any glass he found on the table. There was little or no difference in his usual activity.

In the second week of January, winter showed its true colors with bitter cold and snow, a turnaround from the previous week. During this time the pair made regular visits to the feeder in the pear tree and the one on the deck railing. Mr. Jay Jay continued his daily excursions with his demanding mate, but still returned home every evening for the comforts of food and a warm perch. There were some noticeable changes taking place in his behavior. He showed less and less interest in his toys, and his usually sociable attitude became increasingly indifferent. My baby jay was growing up.

Amazingly, he had sustained his dual existence in two entirely different worlds while successfully pairing up with a free female. I really wished that I could understand bird talk and hear the story of what Miss Jay thought of a suitor who abandoned her every night for the house. There was no question in my mind about her claim to Mr. Jay Jay.

Whatever she thought of his fraternizing with humans, it didn't keep her from insisting on his attention early every morning. On January 14, Miss Jay was unusually noisy demanding his presence as if he was a bit tardy for their date. She was most obviously upset. I opened the door and he was out in a flash without even a goodbye "Jaeeh." They only had eyes for each other. They were drifting back and forth in the apple trees on the lane, paying no attention to me as I drove off to work.

That evening, I came home anticipating a jay greeting. The house was silent, and I quickly moved through each room searching for him. Then I went outside and called to my jay. Nothing. Darkness settled in without a peep or flutter of wings from Mr. Jay Jay. The cold was extreme that night and I was obsessed with a growing fear. Could he adapt to cold winter nights and living in the open after a sheltered life?

The next morning was shockingly cold and by mid-day the leaden skies were spitting snow. There was still no sign of my pet. I bundled up and went outside to replenish the bird food, all the time hopefully watching for the jays. All types of birds came to the feeders but not a single blue jay. I ventured out to the rock garden and the surrounding area, but not a trace. I sat by the window most of the day—feeling like a mother whose son had just declared his independence.

The morning after the storm was as clear as crystal. Brilliant sunlight on the ten inches of new-fallen snow created a sparkling wonderland. During the day I kept my vigilance at the feeding stations, seeing many different species, but not one single jay. From the beginning, I'd known that someday this incredible and delightful episode would end. Not knowing exactly what had occurred was what distressed me the most. Many disturbing scenarios played out in my mind, intensifying my concern.

The winter marched on toward spring with each day a little longer than the previous one. I continued to place seed and suet cakes out and watched the hordes of birds that came to feast, but still no jays. This was also the time of the year I cleaned and prepared the bird houses for the spring arrivals. After cleaning, the houses received a light dusting with five percent Sevin dust. It is safe to use around birds and reduces the insect problems. Even though Mr. Jay Jay was out of sight he was not out of mind.

Chapter Eight

Reflections

Five weeks had passed without a glimpse of Mr. Jay Jay or any other jay. I tried to turn my thoughts to vegetable gardening and spring cleaning, but then I found his coin tucked in the window and my mind wandered back to my beloved pet. I wanted to believe that he was still alive.

After the weather improved in late February, I went back to the rock garden in search of a clue. The only thing that I found was one blue jay feather underneath one of the juniper plants. That particular area had always been one of his favorite hangouts.

I vividly remembered that just prior to the January snowstorm I had seen the pair turning and raking leaves aside as they hunted for insects. I also recalled that I had seen a stray cat sneaking about the yard and gardens. With that idea in mind, I briefly thought that the cat had been at the root of Mr. Jay Jay's disappearance. Later, I concluded that one jay feather was not sufficient evidence to convict the cat of such a dastardly deed.

A friend of mine, a renowned and avid bird watcher, stopped by for a visit one afternoon. I told her about Mr. Jay Jay and his "leaving the family nest." Knowing she was an expert, I asked her about the migration of blue jays. She reassured me that they do migrate to a slightly warmer climate when severe weather is a threat, but then return home. A research trip to the library verified that blue jays do tend to move somewhat south when the home base gets a little too chilly, but they return to the same area with the seasonal change. This renewed my hope that I would see Mr. Jay Jay again.

With the passing of each day, there was more and more evidence of spring's arrival. Maple trees were red with blooms and the daffodils nodded in the early March wind. Those first warm days and yellow blooms bursting forth turned my thoughts to when the migrating Mr. Jay Jay might return. My feathered assembly of summer residents began to arrive, but still no blue jays.

My anticipation of Mr. Jay Jay's spring homecoming was intermingled with concern over whether he survived re-entry into his natural world. I knew he was intelligent and had certainly demonstrated his ability to adapt as a foster family member. Knowing how contented he had been with his life with us, I trusted he would follow his instincts and reappear soon.

Chapter Nine

Homecoming

By the third week of March, the earlier sunrise and the longer days became more noticeable. I awoke to a glorious day watching glowing bands of color thicken and blend together in the eastern sky. A golden, rosy blush extended as high as the magnificent oak trees that stood near the site of an old chapel across the field. I watched as the sun climbed above the treetops, just appreciating the morning's display of the miracle of creation. The clear, sweet coos of doves sounded across the field as a cardinal trilled in a rich full voice closer to the house. I was really straining my ears for the noisiest and most raucous of birds, but there was no sound of the rowdy blue jays.

It was the first of April and Mother Nature seemed reborn. The gathering of birds in the back yard proudly showed off their vivid plumage, sang their sweetest melodies, and engaged in their mating rituals. As usual, I spent the day at work in my florist shop. Returning home I drove past wet areas listening to spring peepers as the frogs, too, sang their song. Arching crabapple trees, clad in soft pink blossoms, greeted me as I drove up the lane.

After pulling into my parking spot, I simply sat for a while admiring the beauty surrounding me, enlivened by the tantalizing perfume of the hyacinths. Finally, I ended my reverie and left the car, to be startled by the distinctive call of a blue jay. I heard a series of excited "Jaeeh, Jaeeh" calls and began to scan the sky and trees.

I walked slowly toward the house, passing under the cherry tree nearest the patio, when I heard the flutter of wings. It was a pair of blue jays, the first I had seen since January 14, the day of Mr. Jay Jay's departure. I stopped dead in my tracks, and immediately called out a loud "Jaeeh" greeting.

Looking up, the pair of jays appeared to be suspended in space. Maybe, just maybe, my adopted bird had returned home with Mrs. Jay Jay. My heart filled in anticipation of the joy his return would bring.

I moved forward, taking a few tentative steps toward the trees where they had alighted. One of the jays lifted its crest. Was it a sign of alarm or recognition? I again voiced a loud "Jaeeh" greeting. Instantly, one of the jays swooped to within three inches of my shoulder. Instead of landing, the whirring mass of feathers shifted into upward flight and settled down on the low limb of the oak tree just above my head. Knowing that those were abnormal actions for a wild bird, my hopes lifted as I watched the pair begin to flit from limb to limb, staying in close proximity.

Could it really be Mr. Jay Jay or was I reading into this action something that did not exist? All of a sudden there was a string of raucous "Jaeeh, Jaeeh" calls as the jay again sailed to within inches of my head. I recognized the second set of calls as the distinctive greeting of my blue jay. There was no doubt in my mind; the boy was home, even though he was a little shy after a winter's absence.

He let me know he was an adult now, but instinct and the desire for the old home place had won. The mating season had just begun and Mr. and Mrs. Jay Jay settled in near the family, but on their own.

Epilogue

Although I would eagerly await the arrival of my feathered grandchildren, when Mr. Jay Jay returned with his bride on April 3 he had fundamentally reverted to a wild bird. The pair of jays spent most of their time in the woods behind my house, making occasional trips to the bird feeder and later with their offspring. Alas, I had no way of knowing where the nest was located or how many fledglings they had hatched. Mr. Jay Jay never came into the house after he returned home. But that didn't mean our home was birdless.

Three weeks after Mr. Jay Jay first left I bought my first parrot. My fascination with birds continued to grow and I bred and hand raised African Gray Congo parrots for ten years. I kept one of my babies, Tinker Bell, who is now 12 years old and my beloved companion.

About the Author

Dorothy Hickson Dunn, a native of Halifax County Virginia, was educated at Mary Washington College and the University of Virginia with a degree in art. Her career was in floriculture and horticulture in Louisa County.

She is an avid bird enthusiast with 40 years experience in breeding and hand rearing exotic birds and more recently African Gray Congo parrots.

Her hobbies include gardening, landscape painting, gem, mineral and fossil collecting.

ISBN 1-41204161-9

9 781412 041614